HUMAN HORIZONS SERIES

HELPING THE AGGRESSIVE CHILD

How to Deal with Difficult Children

ALAN TRAIN

A Condor Book
Souvenir Press (E&A Ltd)

To my wife Vivienne
and our children
Jonathan, Peter, Helen, Matthew

Vincit qui patitur: G.S.I.

First published 1993 by Souvenir Press
(Educational & Academic) Ltd,
43 Great Russell Street, London WC1B 3PA
and simultaneously in Canada

Reprinted 1995

ISBN 0 285 63152 7

Photoset by Rowland Phototypesetting Ltd,
Bury St Edmunds, Suffolk

Printed in Great Britain by
The Guernsey Press Co. Ltd, Guernsey, Channel Islands

Contents

Part One

UNDERSTANDING AGGRESSION IN CHILDREN

1 Aggression: What is it and Where Does it Come From?

If you are a parent with a highly aggressive child in your family, or if you are a teacher or child care worker who has to deal with severe temper tantrums, you will have experienced the bewilderment and confusion which we all face when confronted with a small human being who is beyond our control.

Most of us feel at a complete loss when a child who is capable of being cooperative, happy and lovable suddenly changes into an unpredictable and fearsome threat. Our hearts sink, breathing becomes difficult, we feel the blood drain from our arms and legs and, invariably, in our confusion we say and do things which we later regret. We feel ashamed that as parents or professionals we don't know what to do—or that the whole sorry mess is in some way our own fault. If we allow our natural reactions to surface, we later feel guilty about acting in what may seem an uncontrolled way. If we do nothing the child inflicts more abuse on us and we become even more frustrated.

We should take consolation from the knowledge that many adults have experienced this situation, and that few have come to any firm conclusions about the best way to deal with the problem. Most, whether they are parents or professionals, just muddle through. The results are broken marriages, divided families or short-lived careers—this is without mentioning the fate of the children themselves.

Some people are able to work very effectively with difficult children. They often have a natural way with them, an intuitive knowledge of the right approach to take when a severe outburst of aggression occurs. It would be hard for the rest of us to learn all their skill because it is so subtle and beyond analysis, but there is some action we can take that will enable us to handle some very difficult situations. In the second part of this book I shall be suggesting practical strategies which others have found very useful, but in Part One I want to present you with some important ideas for consideration.

It is probable that you have already discussed numerous ideas and approaches with child psychologists, social workers and other professionals. You may say that none of these ideas has worked. In your frustration you may even go so far as to say that the professionals seem to need the ideas more than the children do. They certainly provide them with a living!

However, I would like you to consider this question: when you have found yourself in any situation where an instant decision had to be made, how have you arrived at it?

Your instant, out-of-the-blue-decision was probably based on everything you had experienced in the past, either directly or indirectly. By this I mean that whatever you decided was the result of what had happened to you or around you, or of what you had read or seen on television about other people's experiences and ideas. We subtly absorb all our life experiences, and the moment of intuition—when we take that action which we may later regret and feel guilty about—is the result of our total living experience.

It is important, therefore, to recognise that, should you be having difficulty in dealing with a child, it may be that you need to prepare yourself a little better. You may need to look more closely at yourself rather than the child. This may seem quite the wrong way round, but I would suggest that, when you have done this, you will begin to feel stronger in yourself and more able to cope with your difficult child. We shall focus on this in Part Two, Chapter 2.

Initially, however, we need to examine the ideas that other people have had about the nature of this nebulous but potentially explosive force which we call aggression. This is at the centre of everything: once you have begun to think about the nature of aggression, you will have taken the first step towards controlling it, either in yourself or in your aggressive child. You will already be looking at it from the outside, treating it as a human phenomenon in which you need not necessarily become involved. You will be looking at the matter objectively.

Do not therefore be tempted to miss out this part of the

book and go straight to Part Two. This part is essential reading. When you have read it you will have absorbed some very basic ideas and, whether you like it or not, they will have become a valuable part of your repertoire.

As an enthusiastic practitioner I have found it impossible to consider difficult behaviour without immediately suggesting solutions. Although Part Two will concentrate on these, a number of useful guidelines on approaches to treatment naturally follows the consideration of issues covered in Part One.

As you read, I hope that you will find yourself formulating practical solutions of your own, for these will always work better than ideas suggested by others, especially if they have grown out of a wide range of experience and reading.

You may have a particular child in mind, who could benefit from your interest in reading this book. You could be the most important person in his life. He cannot control matters—no matter how you may feel about this! He is relying on someone else to sort things out. If you want to be the one to do this you need to lay some firm foundations for your approach.

One of the oldest debates about human beings is whether they are as they are because of the way they have been brought up, or because they have been born like that—the 'nature versus nurture' controversy. Although the decisions we make in life are based on what we have experienced, there is another factor involved. How many families do you know in which there are three or four children who are well adjusted and another one who is extremely difficult to handle? Time and time again it seems to happen that, despite enjoying the same family life, there is one child who reacts very differently to the attention and love of his parents.

It is true that each child experiences different conditions because of his or her rank in the family, but such remarkable differences as can be found in the children we are talking about cannot be fully explained in this way. Perhaps we should conclude that everyone is born with his own personality which is quite unique and which reacts differently to happenings around him.

Is your aggressive child as he is because he was brought up in a certain way, or was he born like this? Was he a difficult child from the very beginning? Did he react differently from other children in the family? Was he always aggressive? Your answers to these questions will determine your approach.

If you believe that it is the way we bring up our children that makes them aggressive, then to avoid this you should examine how the child has been brought up and attempt to make necessary changes. If you believe that children may be born with an unusually high degree of aggression as part of their make-up, then you will see your role as helping your child to cope with his aggression. You may even go so far as to consider whether his condition requires medical treatment.

During the last hundred years these issues have been debated by some of the most brilliant minds of the day. Let us look at their theories in more detail.

INSTINCTS

We have all marvelled at the way in which a newly born calf or kitten knows exactly where to find its first meal, or the way in which a small baby knows how to get attention without being able to speak. They instinctively know how to survive. The necessary actions and reflexes are built in at birth. Some theorists believe that human beings are born not only with physical reflexes but with other quite separate qualities. They have a hunting instinct and a fighting instinct; they have an inborn desire to acquire things, to compete, to sympathise. They have a natural tendency to imitate, and they feel fear.

From this point of view, the highly aggressive child is seen as someone who has been born with a strong aggressive instinct which forms a dominant part of his make-up.

What do we mean by the aggressive instinct? Some see aggression as a force held back by sluice gates, which occasionally bubbles over. Others see it as a form of energy, like gas in a chamber: now and then it may be released in varying doses. Another view holds that aggression can be likened to an energy that has accumulated to the point where it explodes. It is highly volatile, spontaneous and dangerous because of its unpredictability.

Some believe that human beings have a natural death instinct, an inborn impulse to destroy themselves, to release themselves from the tensions of life. This conflicts with their equally important need to create and preserve life. Aggression may then be interpreted as the result of the death instinct being blocked by the instinct for self-preservation.

In all these theories, however, we can see a common theme: aggression is not a reaction to things that happen around a person, but an innate, uncontrollable impulse. Human beings are born with an aggressive instinct.

If you think about the aggressive child you know, would you say that his behaviour is unpredictable, and that the aggression which frightens you when he explodes seems to come from nowhere? If you have experienced a violent episode you may well feel that these *instinctivists* have got it right, that aggression should be regarded as a powerful, uncontrollable impulse.

It is not only the theorists of the past who believed that aggression is a built-in feature of human beings. Neurophysiologists have advocated psychosurgery as a solution to violent behaviour; other specialists have concluded that aggressive responses in teenage boys can be accounted for by their testosterone levels.

Some researchers believe that various parts of the brain control such impulses as aggression or flight; they claim that outbursts of rage can be activated or inhibited by electrical stimulation. They see aggression as a state of equilibrium, with the activating and inhibiting parts of the brain maintaining a balance. Electrical stimulation or disease alters the circuitry of the brain and the result is an outburst of aggression.

If you find these theories abhorrent, you might be able to accept the idea that your child is 'ill' and needs some form of medication, but despite your sense of total frustration with your difficult child, you are probably hoping for a different kind of solution. Drug therapy must always be regarded as a last resort.

Let us look a little further.

BEHAVIOUR

There is another group of experts who believe that all actions are determined by life experience. The aggressive child is aggressive because of his experience of life and his upbringing. These *behaviourists* believe that human beings always act in their own interests and that it is therefore possible to shape and control behaviour. If you want a child to behave in a certain way, you reinforce the behaviour by rewarding him. When he behaves badly you extinguish the behaviour by disregarding it. A child is aggressive because whenever he has been so people have paid him attention, and thus reinforced the aggression. If he receives attention only when he is not being aggressive, he will become more sociable.

Aggressive outbursts are seen by some behaviourists as the result of frustration. If a child wants to do something and is prevented, the result will be an aggressive outburst, which may take the form of physical or verbal violence. It is this kind of aggression that causes most anxiety. If we are physically threatened we must do something, if only to protect ourselves. If a child screams abuse at us it is equally hard to take, for a harsh verbal attack may seem a threat to our psychological security, especially if it comes from our own child.

On the other hand, a child may show his frustration by retreating into a world of fantasy. This kind of inward-looking aggression is often tolerated more readily, if not completely ignored, since it poses no threat to anyone. A child who continually daydreams, however, should be regarded with concern. His aggression could lead to self-mutilation or even suicide.

Behaviourists would say that we need to be frustrated in order to achieve in life, and that therefore we all have a capacity to tolerate frustration. The intensity of a child's aggression is seen as being directly related not only to the level of his frustration, but also to his perceived sense of injustice or rejection. The implication is that if a child has an outburst of aggression we should look carefully at the way he thinks. What is important to us may be totally irrelevant to him. His outburst may be a reaction to being frustrated in his attempt to achieve some objective of which we are totally unaware.

COMPROMISE

Probably you will compromise and say that your aggressive child was like that from an early age, but that you can also think of a number of events which could have made him worse.

This is the position assumed by another group of experts, collectively known as *psychoanalysts*. They believe that a person's character is a combination of his unique personality and his experience of the world.

Humans, according to this theory, are born with certain qualities, and difficulties experienced in life can create characteristics such as stubbornness or tidiness. They have an inbuilt tendency towards love, and a tendency to destruction. These tendencies, or impulses, vary at birth from child to child. From the beginning of life, however, the child also interacts with the world around him.

You may agree with this theory. You may say that it is impossible to take a hard line and to claim that your child is aggressive and difficult only because he was born that way. You know that things have happened in your own life that have affected the way you behave; it would therefore seem logical to propose that your difficult child has been born with a personality rather more fragile than most, and that he has found it difficult to cope with life. His high degree of frustration is seen in outbursts of aggression. People react to his behaviour with equal intensity and it is reinforced.

A CHILD'S NEEDS

If you feel that you have not met the needs of your child and that he is aggressive because of the way you have brought him up, you should always balance this with the idea that each human is unique and that your child is quite separate from you. He was born with his own personality and you can only accept this and help him to cope with his aggression. However, if you are strong enough to admit that you may have made mistakes with him, it would be invaluable to assess these more systematically. Should you have other children you may then bring them up differently; should you be determined to have no more after this one, a closer look might change your mind! In any case, considering further ideas will enable you to cope with your present problem more effectively.

We constantly hear of children with special needs, and it is worth mentioning that we all have special needs if we are to avoid becoming highly aggressive or withdrawn. Consider these needs which, if not met, may result in children presenting you with difficult behaviour:

1   The need to have a clear picture of the world
A child needs to feel that he has certain people in his life who will always be there. Certain events must always occur; certain rules must always apply. He must know where he stands in relation to everything around him. He needs a map of his personal world, one which can be recognised and one where the compass points do not change. He needs to be able to find his way.

2   The need to have an objective in life
A child needs to have a level of expectation to work to. He needs to know that there are certain rules that are beyond him, that cannot be questioned. He needs to sense that there are certain objectives for him to achieve. These objectives need to be in the interests of others, not just himself.

3   The need to feel part of things
A child needs to feel a sense of relatedness. He needs to be able to see himself as part of a whole. He needs to sense that he is of value to others, that he is part of a network of relationships, a network that gives him a sense of his identity. He needs to belong.

4   The need for stimulation
A child needs stimulation. This will help to develop his language and his capacity for abstract thought. It will also help him to develop his inner controls. Severe boredom can lead to severe problems: children have been known to mutilate

THE NEEDS OF CHILDREN

A CLEAR PICTURE OF THE WORLD

AN OBJECTIVE IN LIFE

TO FEEL PART OF THINGS

STIMULATION

ROOTS

LOVE

themselves or even kill others in an attempt to feel a sense
of their existence.

5   The need for a sense of rootedness
A child needs to bond with his mother. This happens in the
very early stages of childhood and provides an anchor point
for future development. With this foundation he can become
a separate person with a sense of independence, free will
and self-control. If the bonding does not take place with his
mother or another significant person, he may later attempt
to form a similar relationship with others and either try to
control them (sadism) or be controlled by them (maso-
chism). He may become excessively fond of himself or have
a craving to destroy.

6   The need for love
The sense of love, of unconditional acceptance, is built into
the bonding process with a child's mother; we also believe,
however, that it can be achieved in a slightly different form
with others. Unconditional acceptance is not the only necessary component. It is just as important to recognise that love
means caring, and that caring means trying to provide all
the needs which we have already mentioned.

Ask yourself how far these needs have been met in your
particular child. It will help you enormously if you can find
the answer. If you are the parent of an aggressive, difficult
child you will benefit by accepting the part you may have
played in causing problems for him. You should feel good
about being able to do this—most people block out the
truth and the child suffers because of their hidden guilt. You
should also be comforted by the knowledge that life treats
us all differently and that there were probably many circumstances which were well beyond your control.

If you are a professional dealing with other people's children you should appreciate what a complicated business it
is to bring up a child. It may be easy for some parents who
have the time and resources to pay attention to their children, but for others their focus in life must often be the very
basic need we all have, for food and shelter.

This may seem an overstatement, but social scientists have

found, for example, that there is a direct link between the level of criminal violence and economic recession. Young adults who are unable to get jobs and a feeling of status in society are likely to be highly aggressive. Low wage settlements and poor housing conditions, which promote gross overcrowding or isolation, also result in aggression. The more resources a person has at his disposal, the less likely he is to become aggressive.

It is worth pausing a moment to consider the stress experienced by your aggressive child because of family arguments over money. Few families avoid this problem. The more material belongings they have, the more they want. But in some families the level of frustration at not being able to provide even for basic needs frequently leads to violence.

Violence tends to occur in the family environment because of the informal setting it provides for free expression. Money problems or work problems may originate outside the home, but the angry aggression is only expressed within its four walls.

Many people in our society feel a sense of helplessness. They are at the mercy of economic and social forces over which they seem to have no control. Children therefore often grow up in an atmosphere of violence and find it difficult to adjust to the pattern of behaviour expected in the school or community. They act in the only way they know how: they are aggressive, hostile and demand attention in an exhausting way. They are unsettled and unhappy. They are restless, unable to concentrate and extremely volatile. They will attack you either physically or verbally if you threaten them in any way.

Let us look at the way we all act when we are threatened.

BEING THREATENED

We all use certain techniques when we feel threatened. If someone throws a chair at us we will duck to avoid it, or if our reflexes are particularly sharp we may throw it back on the rebound!

But there are other, non-physical situations, where we use more subtle mechanisms. We react with these sophisticated techniques when someone attacks the image we have of

THREAT

WHEN A CHILD FEELS THREATENED HE MAY REACT WITH

PHYSICAL AGGRESSION

SHOULD HE BE ABLE TO CONTROL THIS HE MAY

USE VERBAL AGGRESSION OR SARCASM

DISTORT INFORMATION TO SUIT HIS PURPOSE

AVOID WHAT HE DOES NOT WANT TO HEAR

DISPLAY BIZARRE BEHAVIOUR

HE IS FRAGILE AND VULNERABLE

THESE ARE HIS DEFENCE MECHANISMS

ourselves. It is vital for us to protect our self-image. If we were to lose this, we would be insane.

If we have a strong image of ourselves, if we know who we are and what part we play in a clearly defined world, then we can resist attack. If, however, we are unsure of ourselves, if our self-image is weak, then we will interpret many interactions as a threat and react aggressively.

Broadly speaking, there are three techniques which we use to defend ourselves:
1 We counter-attack with verbal aggression or sarcasm.
2 We distort information to suit our purpose.
3 We avoid what we do not want to hear.

When we think of the aggressive child we should see him as a person who is particularly vulnerable. He is likely to react in a defensive way to much that is said to him.

Because he is smaller than we are (at least when he first starts out), he not only reacts with verbal aggression, he may physically assault us. He will distort information which may be unacceptable to him. Much of what we say about his friends will be interpreted as criticism and felt as a threat. It is his world we are attacking, and he will defend it.

Often he will avoid situations which pose a threat. He may refuse to go to school or to the Cub Scouts; he may hold back his feelings; he may not express himself for fear of destroying the world as he knows it. He may avoid issues in the most obvious way, by withdrawing into his own world of apathy or fantasy, or he may act in a way which is seemingly totally bizarre and unrelated to any threat that you may perceive. In this way he will be displacing his feelings.

No matter how alien his behaviour may appear, it is worth remembering that he is not a creature from another planet! We all have the same essential characteristics, but the fact is that everyone has been dealt a different hand in the personality stakes. Difficult children are endowed with a particularly high degree of sensitivity and their defensive reactions are accordingly severe.

ANGER

Many children have temper tantrums. In young children these are accepted as normal behaviour and dealt with. The

behaviour usually disappears because it is easily ignored.
We are concerned with a child whose outburst of aggression is in quite another league. When this child has a tantrum it is impossible to ignore, if only for your personal safety! The aggression surfacing in these instances has another quality—it has been described as angry aggression.
This is not the same as the aggression we need in order to survive. Normally we are aggressive either when we want to defend ourselves, or when we need to acquire such things as food. In angry aggression, however, we are emotionally aroused; in extreme instances the reward for our aggression may be in the hurt itself which we inflict on the other person.

Highly aggressive children may well be acting aggressively in an attempt to experience a sense of existing. The reactions they receive from those around them will reinforce the behaviour, and consequently they come to associate hurting people with the pleasurable experience of social interaction. This may be the only way they know of reaching out to others.

Cases of aggression like these are extremely difficult to deal with. The more vulnerable the children are the more they will express angry aggression and the more intense and severe will be their reaction.

Let us look at some of the 'triggers' which usually account for such outbursts. There are three main reasons why a child reacts aggressively:

1 When he feels that his objectives are being thwarted.
2 When anyone criticises him or his friends.
3 When he feels that a situation is unjust, or that someone has been negligent or careless.

It is worth emphasising that children examine motives when deciding whether a situation is unjust or not. If your intention is felt to be unfair then their anger will be aroused.

Children should be able to express their anger in an acceptable way. If they are unable to do this their frustration at not being able to achieve their objectives will result in an angry outburst. Many children are taught to overcontrol their anger rather than express it in an acceptable way. If you wish to help a child avoid feeling frustrated you should teach him how to express his thoughts and how to negotiate. It is often wrongly assumed that all children are able to

TRIGGERS

WHEN A CHILD FEELS THAT

HIS OBJECTIVES ARE BEING THWARTED

HE IS BEING CRITICISED

HE IS TREATED UNFAIRLY

HE WILL REACT WITH

ANGER

negotiate—that it is a natural instinct. Should a child not
have had the opportunity to interact with others, or should
he have been exposed to a pattern of aggressive interactions,
then he will most definitely need to be taught these skills.

CONCLUSION

I hope it is becoming clear that there are several different
approaches you can adopt when dealing with your difficult
child. We have only touched on these, but the ideas about
aggression which I have mentioned must have prompted you
to begin noting a few pointers for the practical approach in
Part Two.

Firstly, there is the theory that we are born with built-in
instincts, including aggression. Perhaps you feel that your
role when dealing with an aggressive child is to help him cope
with his condition. Have you considered how you would do
this? Would you begin by having him medically examined?
This would certainly do no harm. You may discover that he
has a condition which makes it difficult for him to hear, or
to see. Do you feel that you will be able to teach him how
to manage his aggression, to live with it, as a diabetic or
epileptic would live with his condition?

Then there is the idea that we can help an aggressive child
by rewarding his good behaviour and paying little attention
to his unacceptable outbursts. Is this really possible in your
case, or would it be unsafe to ignore the aggression when it
occurs? Perhaps it may be possible to take this approach by
thinking very carefully about the setting you provide for him.
It may be that his environment should alter considerably to
suit his needs, rather than your continuing to insist that he
fit in to the setting you have provided. His setting includes
not only his physical surroundings, but his whole life-style.
Your expectation levels may also need close scrutiny. The
guiding principle is to think of his needs, not yours.

Finally, we examined the way in which we all try to defend
ourselves and we recognised that vulnerable children do this
more than others. We looked at the idea of angry aggression
and reduced its triggers to three broad categories. Practical
suggestions immediately come to mind:

If we can talk to a child at the beginning of a day or a

lesson and discuss in simple terms what his plans are, and if we can make sure that he is not frustrated in achieving them, we shall go a long way towards avoiding aggressive outbursts.

If we can respect him and his friends and pay attention to his sensitivity in this area, we shall again avoid a negative reaction.

If we explain very clearly and simply the ground rules for his behaviour, and if we are consistent in our application of them, we shall prevent him feeling that an injustice has occurred and he will not react with aggression.

Above all, if we can maintain our objective, which is to understand and help him, he will sense our investment and never question our intent. He will be unlikely to react with aggressive outbursts.

If we can minimise the number of aggressive outbursts that a child has, and give him praise, encouragement and attention at other times, he will begin to learn how to relate to us in a positive, pleasurable way. His unwanted behaviour will be extinguished.

2 Aggression in Childhood

Parents and professionals are often unsure whether or not they should be concerned about a child's behaviour. Although there is a general pattern to childhood development, individual children develop at different rates and in different directions; there is always, therefore, the temptation to presume that a child will naturally grow through any problems.

If you are the parent of a child who has severe outbursts of aggression, or a teacher or child care worker who has to manage such behaviour, you will realise the need to be realistic about the situation. Many parents and professionals avoid facing up to the issue until it is too late. They have a nagging suspicion that all is not well, but because of their personal investment in the child they repress any lurking thought that he is presenting difficulties, fearing that his behaviour might be seen as a reflection on them. If he threatens the image they have of themselves their defence mechanism of avoidance usually comes into play. Consequently the child's abnormal behaviour is denied with such remarks as, 'Well, boys will be boys,' or, 'Girls do go through these stages, you know.'

Teachers and child care workers often labour under the assumption that they should be able to manage any child's behaviour. They have a misconstrued perception of what professionalism means and may be unwilling to admit that certain children present them with severe problems.

The situation is not helped by headteachers and psychologists who are reluctant to recognise that there may be cause for concern. Their initial response to an anxious parent or teacher who has sensed the need to do something is very often to say that such behaviour is part and parcel of the maturational process. The suspicion is that they really don't know what to do about such children; that they are hoping that if they wait long enough the child's aggressive behaviour will go away. Frustrated parents are frequently faced with inaction—pseudo-professionalism. They would feel far more support if they knew that someone else found the child difficult to comprehend and manage. Meanwhile the child's behaviour deteriorates even further as he interprets inaction as either lack of external control or a condoning of his aggression. The behaviour of a child is always reinforced by tacit acceptance.

Unwanted behaviour can be further reinforced by an intensive reaction from the adult, who may do all he or she can to avoid confronting the behaviour. For a long time incidents may have been tolerated. But resentment accumulates as the adult, in an attempt to avoid the stigma attached to having a difficult child, persuades him- or herself that the child is just going through a phase. The necessary intervention, which would indicate to the child that there was somebody who cared about him and would give him a sense of being controlled, is therefore not taken.

Inevitably, the day comes when the adult snaps. Feelings of shame, helplessness and rejection are powerfully released. In cases of prolonged stress inflicted on an adult by a child, the damage that is counter-inflicted may be severe. Adults who abuse children cannot believe the potency of their frustration.

Because of the powerful emotions experienced in such confrontations, the mode of behaviour may become persistent and self-reinforcing. It may become part of the child's behavioural repertoire. If it persists into adulthood the likelihood is that it will continue with the next generation.

It is important therefore that whenever parents, teachers or child care workers feel under stress with a child, they take action. They should seek help, and the professionals to whom they turn should recognise that if nothing is done they may well have missed an opportunity to avoid a great deal of trouble later. Supporting each other by listening is a crucial part of any treatment programme.

When we feel under stress with a child, we are often confused about the underlying cause. Is it our own state of mind that needs attention? We may have had a particularly bad day; we may feel that we are getting a little too old.

We should cast such thoughts aside. If we are parents we

should trust our intuition—it is a much undervalued asset; if we are teachers or child care workers, we should recognise that whenever we feel under stress we should take action. It is when we merely plod on that we are being negligent. If we have had a hard day or are finding it difficult to keep up with the child, then we should regard it as especially important to seek help. If we are under any degree of personal stress we will find it impossible to cope positively with an aggressive child.

Let us look at how aggression occurs in normal childhood development. We may then be able to put the child we have in mind into some kind of context; perhaps we shall be better able accurately to assess excessive levels of aggression.

AGGRESSION IN INFANCY

When a child is born he is solely concerned with his own needs. The only thing which is real to him is his person. He has bodily needs, physical feelings, and thoughts. He does not relate to people in an affective way, but views them intellectually as part of the system he needs to survive. At birth his activity is almost synonymous with aggression.

This concern of the child with his own needs is usually accepted by the parent. The subsequent bond between them is considerable. Total acceptance of a purely selfish and non-reciprocating act never occurs at any other time. It is the basis of the love that exists between the parent and the child, and although the intensity of the unique relationship is brief it forms the bedrock of the infant's climb towards maturity and adulthood.

Should the bonding process not take place, the infant's developmental process will be affected. This is not to say that as a result the child will be excessively aggressive in later life. He may well be able to cope admirably. His ability to do so will depend on whether he is emotionally fragile or resilient. In other words, it will depend on his personal make-up at birth.

If you are the parent of an aggressive child, you should think back to the time he was born. No matter how long ago this was, you will undoubtedly remember the very early stages in some detail. Did he cry a lot? Did you find that when you picked him up to comfort him he cried even more? Did you find that it was impossible to give him enough food to keep him quiet? In general, could he have been described as a contented baby or was he always miserable and agitated?

More importantly, however, you should try to remember your own state of mind during the pregnancy and when he was born. Was this a happy time of your life, or was your situation unsettled? The more unsettled and insecure you were, the more difficult you would have found it to cope with this all-demanding, self-centred new human being. The unconditional acceptance of your child would have been impossible. He may not have been able to sense to the full that level of security necessary for development towards independence and personal control.

You should not regard yourself as totally responsible for his present aggressive behaviour. Everyone, including yourself, is at the mercy of his or her life circumstances.

Do not forget that while it is important for you to acknowledge the part your personal state of affairs may have played in your child's development, it is equally important to recognise that there is another person involved here—the infant himself. He was born with strengths and weaknesses, and there was nothing you could do about the unique chemistry of his personality. His tendency to develop inappropriate levels of aggression is based on his personal capacity to cope with the demands of his life.

His aggression may be connected to the nature of his birth and his physical condition. Difficult births may result in some level of organic dysfunction, and physical illnesses in early childhood may promote excessive aggression. A child should be medically examined if he is causing problems of any kind. It may well be that suitable medication can be administered, and that the child's difficulties can be viewed as a condition to be treated. Aggression is sometimes associated with physical and mental disabilities, and should then be regarded as a symptom of frustration. If it is possible to alleviate the primary disability, the tendency to be aggressive will diminish.

AGGRESSION IN CHILDHOOD

Growing in any sense needs a degree of aggression. If we were born without aggression we would be unable to survive the early stages of our life and would not thereafter be able to progress in our development. Aggression comes from an innate tendency to grow and master the world around us. It can be seen as a characteristic of all forms of life.

A common anxiety among parents is that their child is not aggressive enough. They worry that he may not be able to look after himself when he goes to school. They may tell him to retaliate if anyone attacks him, and the level of their anxiety if he does not come out fighting may promote within him a severe sense of rejection. Perhaps the most abused child is one who retreats into a world of fantasy because of such parental demands. The child withdraws farther into his protective shell as he tries to maintain his sense of self-worth. The usual parental reaction is to reject him even more.

This common pattern of adult behaviour has its origins in the knowledge that to survive it is essential for the small human being to be aggressive.

We need aggression to be able to control our environment, for this is how we can become independent. Aggression usually increases the farther we go back towards infancy. As we get older we become more in control and less dependent on others. We feel less threatened and are not so likely to react aggressively.

By the age of twelve months a child begins to display instrumental aggression. This is aggression directed towards playmates and usually involves toys and possessions. The child is beginning to impose himself on his surroundings. His centre of attention begins to be objects in his environment rather than himself. In a way these objects are seen as part of himself: anyone who attempts to take away his toys is regarded as a threat to his identity. The result is an outburst of aggression. This phenomenon, like other human qualities, persists throughout life in various forms: few adults can completely deny the satisfaction of owning things.

As a child approaches his fifth or sixth year his aggression changes in quality. He becomes less likely to use physical violence to achieve his aims, and he will react with anger only if he thinks he is being attacked intentionally.

In the pre-school years he becomes skilled at perceiving the intentions of those around him. This skill develops beyond the point where it is necessary for a verbal exchange to take place before he understands what you are going to do. Before he can speak the child has receptive language— he has the ability to know what you mean when you say something to him. He will be able to assess a situation well before he begins school. It is the intention of a person that may trigger his aggression.

He develops from a child who acts aggressively to acquire what he wants, to a child who only acts aggressively when he feels that someone is threatening him. The degree of threat that he experiences or feels is directly related to his intrinsic level of fragility. This in turn will have been affected by his life circumstances. Thus all children react differently, and perceive intention in a unique way.

KINDS OF CHILDHOOD AGGRESSION

It has been observed in nursery schools that there are three broad categories of aggression in children.

There are those children who, when playing games, become physically wild and out of control. Their aggression is very rough and intimidating but is confined to play situations usually involving fantasy. At other times they are timid, talk relatively little and make few attempts to organise others. They have little success in resolving disputes.

Other children are physically aggressive in disputes and very domineering. They specialise in harassing others and without provocation will repeatedly direct aggression at the same person, continually teasing and threatening. They talk little, and when they do they often whisper. They are among the most aggressive and violent children.

A third group is those children who are aggressive and dominant in their speech but are not physically violent. Their aggression occurs outside the games situation. They are usually regarded by other children as boring because of a pre-occupation with themselves. These children are regarded as being better adapted socially. They have a relatively low level of aggression and show little violence in all situations. They can be persuasive, not just domineering, and although they talk a lot they can be quite interesting. They tend not to be concerned about their relationships with others. These patterns of behaviour usually persist until at least the age of seven or eight years.

AGGRESSION IN BOYS AND GIRLS

The difference between levels of aggression in boys and girls appears in the second year of life. Studies have found that boys are more likely than girls to retaliate with physical aggression when they are attacked or when someone interferes with their objectives. The kinds of aggression observed in nursery schools are more noticeable in boys than in girls. Some would say that boys are more aggressive because of their higher level of activity, which can be attributed to the physical structure of their bodies and the male hormone pattern. Studies reveal that, among all children, boys are more active, overtly aggressive and combative than girls, and they also elicit more aggressive responses from other children. Among boys there is a greater degree of acquisitive competition and they are more retaliatory than girls.

However, it should not be assumed that this pattern of behaviour is entirely biological in origin. It is also believed that the reason boys predominantly react in this way is because they receive far more attention than girls when it comes to their aggressive behaviour. Parents expect them to be more aggressive than girls. Boys will always be encouraged to be 'boys'. Aggression is a masculine stereotype.

Society can be seen to exert an influence on a child's development by its cultural definitions and in particular by the way in which it ascribes roles to men and women. Children are exposed to its traditions from the moment they are born.

In America, where the macho image of man is well recognised, homicide rates are five times as high for males as they are for females, and males commit twenty times as many robberies as women. In countries where cultural roles are more equal, the rates of criminal offences have been observed to begin to equalise between the sexes. It is interesting to note that, as women have become emancipated, so has there been a relative decrease in the differences in delinquency and criminal rates for males and females.

GROWING PAINS

We have already mentioned the advisability of having the difficult, aggressive child medically examined. This applies at any stage in his development. The child who is causing you problems is having them himself and his difficult behaviour could perhaps be quickly remedied by a medical examination.

A child who suddenly begins to have outbursts of aggression may have had an accident. He may have fallen quite severely and banged his head. Many such incidents occur without the knowledge of the parent or teacher. He may begin to be aggressive when he is unable to do his work, and this may be caused by his inability to see or hear properly.

A child often only begins to be excessively aggressive when he starts school and it may be that he finds the work he is given too hard, or that there is another child in his class who poses a threat to him.

It may be that other children have things which he would like, that he feels ashamed of the clothes he has to wear, or that he is heavily teased because of his accent or the fact that he wears glasses.

Perhaps he feels that his teacher is picking on him and that he or she is being unfair in some way.

If he is thwarted in his objectives to succeed in doing the work that the other children do, if he feels that he is criticised too much or sees the intentions of his teacher as unjust, he will react with an aggressive outburst.

These are the kind of triggers we discussed earlier in Chapter 1, and you may be totally unaware that they exist for him.

As he develops there may be further growing pains silently festering. He may have difficulty in coping with his brothers and sisters. Children rarely accommodate each other's weaknesses, and if he is at all vulnerable he will be taunted in quite a subtle way. He may be very sensitive to any stresses in the close dynamics of the family where raw emotions are often released.

GROWING PAINS

MEDICAL:

BIRTH COMPLICATIONS
CHILDHOOD ILLNESSES
PHYSICAL CONDITION
SIGHT
HEARING
INJURIES – KNOWN OR UNKNOWN

SCHOOL:

INABILITY TO DO WORK
AN UNFAIR TEACHER
TEASED BY OTHER CHILDREN

HOME:

STRESSED BY FAMILY DYNAMICS
BORED
LACK OF CONSISTENCY

He may be severely bored and lacking any kind of stimulation. If he is an only child he may be lonely and unable to practise the kind of skills he needs to negotiate and communicate. He may be missing the regular routines of a normal family existence and the consistent presence of adults and children who may become significant to him.

Most children experience these growing pains in some way or other. You can tell by the severity of their behaviour how difficult they are finding it to work through them.

TEMPER TANTRUMS

Unlike much behaviour, the temper tantrum is not learned. At a very early age its purpose is to ensure that the needs of the child are met. In infancy the mother responds to the tantrum, but as the child grows she pays less attention to it, and the child begins to use other ways of communicating.

Children under the age of five years often have tantrums. They destroy their possessions, fight and take things belonging to others. They are disobedient, tell lies and bully. There is usually no cause for concern: the child is going through a complex series of stages towards acceptable methods of negotiation and communication. But if the tantrums are excessively severe and frequent and if they persist beyond this age, then action should be taken.

As a parent you will know when the level of severity has been reached. It will be when you have reached your level of frustration tolerance. This is when you begin to feel that you cannot cope any longer: you are about to explode.

As a teacher or child care worker you will be able to gauge the seriousness of the situation by the amount of attention you have to give to this child alone. If you feel that other children are beginning to suffer because of his behaviour, then he has special needs. In particular, if he is becoming a danger to himself or others you must take action. If you feel under severe stress yourself because of him this will reinforce the urgency for his needs to be assessed.

When the temper tantrum has become unacceptable it is because the demands on you are unacceptable.

It could be that the child has had too much attention— that his every need has been met for too long and that he has not been able to develop. He is perhaps still acting in an infant mode: he has a tantrum because he knows that it will reap a reward.

DIFFICULT CHILDREN

Normal children are significantly more friendly than difficult children; they spend more time in cooperative activities and are eager to share their enjoyment.

If they show aggression it is to protect the smooth running of their cooperative activities and to establish a share in the toys or materials they are using. They tend to be aggressive when they feel threatened, but their aggression dissipates fairly rapidly. They tend to be too involved in their activities to be clinging or whingy. The main purpose of their interactions is the desire to play, to be friendly and to share experience.

Difficult children are more contrary. They are negative and annoying. They are dominating, physical and boastful. Those with an aggressive nature may be quarrelsome, noisy, bossy and quick-tempered; or they may show demanding behaviour and may pester, whine and seek attention. Both these groups of aggressive children are extremely unpopular with their peers.

CONCLUSION

Aggression is an essential part of any child's development. He needs it to survive from the moment he is born. As he grows his aggression changes in its quality. From using aggression to achieve his bodily needs he begins to use it only when he is threatened. As he progresses into adulthood his raw aggression is refined to the point where it is disguised in the form of subtle defence mechanisms which allow him to retain his sense of identity. During adolescence we see a surge towards a sense of self, and we shall discuss this critical stage of development in Chapter 4.

Many of the difficulties presented by young men and women could be avoided by considering their needs during early childhood. We discussed these needs in Chapter 1, and it would be worth reminding yourself of what they are.

Aggression in childhood becomes excessive and inappropriate when these needs are not met.

Perhaps you will already have come to realise that the aggressive behaviour which causes concern is really only a matter of degree. All children are aggressive. It is the inappropriateness of the aggression in relation to the age of the child that creates problems.

A question which you should ask yourself is whether the child you have in mind is much more aggressive than other children in his age group. You could also try to assess whether it is the severity of his outbursts that worries you or whether it is their frequency. By asking such questions you may be able to understand precisely what it is that causes you anxiety. You may also be able to begin to decide on a plan of action.

If your child is more aggressive than all his friends, start by having him medically examined. In particular have his sight and hearing monitored. If all is well, look into the matters I mentioned in relation to other growing pains. It could be that he feels abused by friends or relatives. Decide whether there are any specific triggers for his anger (see Chapter 1). By looking at the circumstances surrounding each episode you may find some constant factor which could then be avoided.

Finally, let me remind you of the three main reasons why a child may react with excessive aggression:

He may react aggressively when he feels that someone is interfering with his objectives.

He may react aggressively when he feels that he or his friends are being criticised.

He may react aggressively when he feels that a situation is unjust, or when he feels that a person has been negligent or careless.

This behaviour is present in all children; it persists in those who are particularly vulnerable.

A simple solution, therefore, would be for you to make sure that you regularly talk to your aggressive child in order to:

1 clarify objectives for both you and him
2 ensure that he does not interpret what you say as criticism, and

3   make the ground rules for his behaviour clear.

We shall be examining the aggressive child's difficulty in communicating in Part Two. It is the frustration he feels in not being able to communicate that can lead to aggressive outbursts.

3 Promoting Aggression

The world of the child does not automatically coincide with yours. You may feel that he fully understands your motives and that it is unreasonable for him not to do so, but you must realise that if this were the case he would already be operating in an adult mode. We do not only develop physically, intellectually and emotionally: our sense of morality and our ethics take a lifetime to mature. You may be able to appreciate why it is wrong for him to set fire to his bedroom; he may not—he may simply have been trying to keep warm.

Very many children, particularly those who are fragile, have had their condition exacerbated by adults who have failed to recognise that they are dealing with children. Adults may become angry when they perceive the intention of a child to be hostile, and this happens all too easily if they regard him as a little adult.

You must of course show your anger when faced with a bedroom that is on fire! The child will feel your response, even though he may not be able to grasp your logical explanation of why it is wrong. Equally, however, you must remember that he is a child, and that he should not feel rejected by you. We shall be discussing how you see yourself and how you see the child in Part Two, Chapter 2.

It is important to be very clear about the intention of a child when he behaves inappropriately, but it is just as important to be clear about your motives when you decide where he should be and what he should be doing. Outbursts of frustration and aggression are often promoted by a distorted perception of intent.

PLAYGROUPS AND NURSERY SCHOOLS

Increasingly, mothers find it necessary to go out to work, and none of them would deny that this causes them anxiety.

Their principal concern is that they may be doing some harm to their child by leaving him with others.

A mother who leaves her child for work has good reason to be concerned. As much time as possible should be spent by parents with a child as he develops through his early years. The mother in particular has a unique bond with him which, if broken prematurely, may harm both the child and herself. The more time she invests in the child in his very early years the more secure he will feel, and the more able he will be to progress towards independence.

A word of caution, though: a great deal of aggression and difficult behaviour is promoted in children by parents who invest in their child too heavily, for too long. These parents will not allow the natural process of separation to take place; they need the child more than he needs them, and their level of indulgence can be extremely harmful.

A mother who must work because of essential financial considerations should do so. Should she be under severe pressures of any kind, her anxiety will be felt by the child and could lead to him becoming the object of her frustrations. She may also need to go out to work because she is simply unable to accept that the child has priority over her career aspirations. The resentment she feels at having to deny herself opportunities will inevitably be transmitted to him.

A clear assessment of needs should be made when parents are deciding whether or not it is 'safe' for the mother to go out to work—the needs of the parents as well as the child. An honest approach should be taken and practical solutions worked out. It is a mistake to presume that only mothers can cater for the needs of a child: there is evidence to support the notion that it is how a child is treated that is the important factor, rather than by whom.

Should both parents work, then arrangements will have to be made for the child to be looked after. The extended family has largely disappeared, but for other reasons many parents prefer their child to attend a playgroup or nursery school. They feel that he will benefit from being with other children of his own age; that by being in a group situation he will be able to learn how to negotiate and to interact generally with others.

In the playgroup and nursery school the child's ability to cope with his aggression in a pro-social way will be considerably developed. If he is alone at home with an adult who is at a completely different developmental stage, his rate of progress will be considerably slower, and in particular a child whose behaviour is difficult can benefit enormously by attending well-supervised playgroups and nursery schools.

He will not only learn how to relate to others, he will feel part of something; he will develop a sense of belonging to a unique group—outside his family. The playgroup and nursery school will also provide him with the opportunity to be stimulated to the level he requires. Boredom can lead to severe behaviour problems.

However, playgroups and nursery schools can actually promote aggression as well as control it. Aggressive behaviour often goes unnoticed by supervisors and passive children are encouraged to be more assertive. It is interesting to note that children tend to imitate aggression in other children rather than aggression in adults: if a child is to learn how to refine his aggression then it is vital for him to experience a group situation where there is a suitable mixture of children. It may be comforting for parents to know that various studies indicate that, in general, children attending playgroups exhibit few problems.

If a child is to benefit from attending a playgroup or nursery school, the parent should be involved as much as possible. Children who are particularly fragile will not find it easy to make the necessary break from their parents. They may feel rejected and unable to cope with the threat of a new situation. Parents should recognise this and become involved in the work of the group, attending regularly in the initial stages. They should not presume that the child can simply be left to get on with it. It may take a number of weeks for this to become a possibility: the child needs time to attach himself to other significant people and the process cannot be hurried.

Even with other people in his life he will still need his original anchor points. Parents should always take a keen interest in what he is doing and should allocate time to talk about the day spent apart, so that the child has every opportunity to crystallise his new, separate life.

Of crucial importance is the child's ability to progress towards being able to read. Inability to read is almost synonymous with problematic behaviour. We cannot escape the fact that literacy skills are an essential requirement in our society.

In these early stages parents and professionals can help enormously by simply reading to a child, and encouraging him to read with them. Paired reading at any age is enjoyable as a shared experience; it is essential if you wish to avoid behavioural difficulties. Many children actually learn to read this way. It is not important to decipher words and to know how to teach reading. You simply read to the child, allowing him to look at the text when he wishes. If you enjoy doing this, he will automatically absorb your enthusiasm. Be careful not to impart any anxiety, for this is what stops us learning. Simply read to him and know that you can only be doing good. He will begin to follow you when he is ready. Be aware that this may take many months.

Do not expect that during your time together he will respond in the loving, passive way you might be hoping for. Remember that he is in his own little world and cannot be expected to appreciate your intentions. He may perceive that you are unwilling to play with him; you may see yourself as tired. He may feel that you are organising him, when all he wants is to play on his own. If you set aside a time for him—and this is surely the best way of arranging matters—appreciate that he needs to do his own thing, not yours. Very often he may prefer you just to be there. If you make inappropriate demands you will promote an aggressive response.

PLAYING AND WAR GAMES

Everyone recognises the importance of children's play. It is during play that a child begins to be able to cope with his world. He exists in his fantasies and only gradually is he able to manage the world around him. In his play he explores his feelings and dissipates his anxieties; he rehearses events in order to control outcomes; he practises his social skills.

It is through play that he develops the capacity to use language and thereafter to think symbolically. If his ability to do this is restricted, then his capacity for effective communication will be limited. He may well become frustrated and excessively aggressive.

During play children are gradually able to become separate from their parents. The bond between a mother and child which enables the child to survive at birth is gradually weakened. As the child grows away he uses transitional supports—objects with which he identifies. They become almost as much a part of him as his mother was, but he relies on them less as he finds ways of relating to others. This developmental path towards a separate self is eased through the process of play.

A concern of some adults is that by allowing children to have certain transitional objects they are not encouraging development to take place. These cuddlies—like the favourite blanket that is carried everywhere and needed especially at night—are often taken away prematurely. When the child is ready he will do without them, and to deny him this support can only cause problems.

Play is essential to any form of development. However, parents and professionals are sometimes concerned that by allowing a child to indulge in war games and play with toy knives and guns they may be promoting aggression. Studies have shown that children's war games promote no more aggression than other games and that children can be as aggressive with a teddy bear as they can be with a toy gun.

Having said this, the indications are that if a child is aggressive to begin with he is likely to become more so if the opportunity arises.

When we discussed the nature of aggression in Chapter 1, a concept mentioned was that it is a powerful, innate force. Unless its energy is released there is an explosion. This cathartic effect is presumed by many people to be a valuable asset of play; however, the concept is disputed by many theorists and practitioners.

Studies have shown that aggressive children who are told stories with an aggressive theme and then given toys which lend themselves to aggressive play become more aggressive than children who are told neutral stories and given non-aggressive toys. Adults who take children swimming or to play football in order to dissipate their aggression often find that it has been increased. The expression of aggression, on the basis of these findings, has no consistent tendency to reduce it, and will have the opposite effect on a child with a naturally aggressive personality.

When thinking of play activities for a child you should therefore be clear about his needs. If he tends to be aggressive you will be doing him no good service if you provide a setting that will stimulate his violent behaviour. The release of aggression may appear to work—but when you try to assume control you will find that its effect is short-lived. The aggressive child should be placed in a non-aggressive setting where he can experience pleasure. He may then begin to operate in a more passive mode.

You will be able to assess whether a child is benefiting from a game by his level of control during play: you will have a second check on this by looking at his rate of recovery afterwards. If he takes a long time to begin to operate in an acceptable way the activity will have been unsuitable. You should opt for a game that will dampen his energies and have a stabilising effect.

Try to give an aggressive child every opportunity to go through the process of play, even if you have to provide special facilities. You will be aware of how he reacts to different toys and games. If you are uneasy about whether they are increasing his aggression, try offering something completely different and measure in your own mind whether you feel more comfortable. As an adult, trust in your intuition—do not be bound to a set approach. If you have made an accurate assessment of your child's level of aggression you will be able to provide the right kind of toys and games for him. You must take control in this way and decide what play facilities will be available. If aggressive toys and games are not provided he will be denied the opportunity to stimulate his aggression; if you give him a choice he will choose to play aggressively.

Most of the work you are able to do with an aggressive child centres around minimising the possibility of an outburst. The longer he can operate in a non-aggressive way, the more his new behaviour will be reinforced.

EXPOSING

AN

AGGRESSIVE CHILD

TO

AGGRESSIVE ACTIVITIES

AGGRESSIVE STORIES

AGGRESSIVE FILMS

COMPETITIVE GAMES

WILL INCREASE

HIS AGGRESSION

TELEVISION AND FILMS

Many adults are concerned about aggression and violence on television and the impact it has on children. The importance of play in this respect cannot be over-emphasised. During play children indulge in fantasies which enable them to cope with the world outside themselves. If they have had the opportunity to do this, they are more able to distinguish between fantasy and reality. Generally, the more secure a child is in relation to his real world, the more he is able to tolerate and even enjoy aggressive fantasy.

Younger children are the most susceptible to the influence of television, perhaps because of their inexperience in distinguishing between fantasy and reality. Another group likely to be at risk is older delinquents who are perhaps frozen in a world of fantasy, where fictional events are as real as anything else.

Children will always tend to imitate behaviour that is an exaggeration of their own style. Thus aggressive children who watch aggressive adults will copy their behaviour, and aggressive children who watch aggression on television will become more aggressive.

The most powerful effect of violence on television is when children are repeatedly exposed to it. Watching scene after scene of aggression and violence diminishes their inhibition and they begin to accept that violent solutions to problems are allowed. It is not easy to be precise about this effect, since it has been found that aggressive children watch television more than other children and prefer violent programmes. Their parents may find that this is an easy way of controlling them, and the process is self-reinforcing for both adults and children.

Although a child may become engrossed in a television programme he is essentially a passive spectator. Should he watch programme after programme he will become immune to stimulation from the world around him; he will become bored by it.

Used selectively, television can be a positive influence, if only because someone is controlling the child's behaviour. The fact that someone else decides when the television is to be used is of crucial importance.

COMPETITIVE SPORTS

Even in a playground or nursery school a child will be encouraged to compete with others.

This can be most unfortunate for the more vulnerable child. He may react aggressively if he is threatened by failure. Regrettably our society has forgotten that before children can compete they have to be strong enough and mature enough to accept that we all have our strengths and weaknesses.

In early childhood especially there should be a great deal of emphasis on individuality. The idea should be inculcated that we are all different, and any move towards the Olympic ideal of *citius, altius, fortius* (swifter, higher, stronger) should be seen in terms of personal progress. In our schools we should teach children that the important thing is not to measure yourself against others but to measure yourself against yourself. Children should be told that when they enter a competition they are there to improve and to help others to do the same.

Competitive sport neither increases nor decreases aggression, but competition increases conflict and may lead to violence. It often promotes negative feelings, especially where the competition is unequal. For a child who has a negative, aggressive attitude it can only be assumed that this will be harmful: he will invariably suffer if he compares himself to others. He has a need constantly to boost his self-esteem, and should he be asked to adopt the aggressive stance promoted by present-day competition it will aggravate his condition.

There is always a tendency to channel aggression into a sport where it can be released in an acceptable way. Evidence suggests, as we have seen, that although this kind of release may happen momentarily, in general terms involvement in an aggressive sport will only promote further aggression in children who are excessively aggressive to begin with.

BULLIES

Most parents will appreciate the need for children to exhibit a degree of aggression, but none will admit that their child is a bully. This is because a bully is universally disliked. He is a person who gains pleasure from a conscious desire to hurt or threaten someone.

It is hard to imagine that small children are capable of being bullies. However, we have seen that in nursery schools a great deal of aggression can take place. Some would say that this aggressive, bullying behaviour has been experienced at home, or by the children being repeatedly exposed to it on television. It has become for them an accepted way of behaving.

Teachers and child care workers will often dismiss children who report bullies; they advise them not to be tell-tales, or they respond with remarks such as, 'Well, you must have deserved it!' The fact that the bully's behaviour is given this form of tacit approval reinforces his way of relating to others.

It is difficult to identify bullies and to decide what may have caused their behaviour, but we know that the toleration of aggressive behaviour in a young child, allied to his parents' indifference and lack of involvement, is a principal factor.

Bullies usually have assertive, aggressive attitudes over which they have little control. They are unable to appreciate the feelings of their victim, and they lack any sense of guilt, often rationalising that the victim deserves the treatment which they have inflicted on him. However, they cannot easily be stereotyped. Some achieve well academically; some appear quite secure and happy.

Likewise, their victims are not always weak, small and shy. They are, however, very vulnerable personalities who find it difficult to withstand physical or verbal attacks. They usually have negative thoughts about themselves; they have a low level of self-esteem and feelings of inadequacy and helplessness. Following lengthy periods of bullying they may become suicidal. Typically, victims may be underachieving at school and absent a great deal; they may appear depressed or have inexplicable outbursts of aggression.

It is important to identify bullies and victims as soon as possible. Some form of action then needs to be taken. Minor incidents should be dealt with before they escalate to a serious condition. Aggression in young children can be more than mere assertiveness, and should the young child be allowed to operate in a deliberately hurtful way he will most likely develop into a delinquent; should a child be consistently bullied he may develop serious psychological problems.

When attempting to deal with bullies it is a good idea to think of them as victims. Usually they are very insecure and have a distorted perception of themselves and others. They may not be able to relate to their peers.

Bullying gangs exist because of the fact that bullies can only connect with their peers through bullying. They have not experienced alternative ways of seeing themselves in relations to others. Victim gangs, of swots and non-physical sports types, can begin to resign themselves to martyrdom.

Very often the bully will feel that he does not fit in. His size—either large or small compared to his peers—may isolate him; he may have learning difficulties which have gone unnoticed; the significant adults in his life may be bullies.

A central part of any intervention should be direct action. Once the bully and the victim are aware that the behaviour is not condoned then the fear of the victim that the bullying will persist will be dissipated; the bully will also be released from his position of control without losing face. The reassurance felt by both bully and victim when it is clear that somebody else is in control is an essential prerequisite for any successful treatment programme.

Both bully and victim should be spoken to separately. In dealing with them it is important to realise that the purpose is to help them see themselves in a different light: you, the adult, are there to strengthen them, not to add fuel to fire. It is extremely easy to promote the bully's image of being a bully and to relate to him in a bullying way; it is easier still to bully the victim in the futile hope that you will shake him into some degree of assertiveness.

The bully will not immediately be able to appreciate an alternative perception of the victim or of the way in which the bullying occurred. He will tend to maintain the perception of himself as a bully. You should nevertheless be firm in your declaration that bullying is not going to be tolerated. You should not attempt to analyse a bullying episode—this will only recreate the scenario for him. The message should

BULLIES

AND

VICTIMS

ARE

VICTIMS

OF

A

DISTORTED
PERCEPTION

OF

THEMSELVES

simply be that such behaviour is not acceptable. The boundaries should be clearly stated, without any form of discussion. He is looking for you to be in control.

However, this will be completely ineffective unless it is followed by some form of acceptance of him as a person. Mistakes happen and it is possible that he was unaware of the way his behaviour affected the other child, or that people disliked him for bullying; he may not have realised that you thought of him as someone who might possibly be a journalist one day, someone who could write, who might make a good sports reporter, and so on. You have heard from another teacher how well he played for the school last week . . . will he be playing on Saturday . . . ? This is how you should talk to him.

You should conclude with a restatement of your initial declaration: that bullying will not be tolerated. You should make sure that he understands what you mean by this—in precise terms related to the most recent episode. The interview should terminate on a note of firmness, fairness and above all confidentiality. To reveal your conversation with him to anyone else would be a breach of the trust he may have begun to place in you.

The victim should feel that in you he has found someone who will listen and empathise. Through you he will gain support from the knowledge that you simply listen and do not ignore. You do not demand that he behave in a way which may be alien to his nature—that he 'give them one back!' You are there to understand.

You are also there to help in a more directive way. What you must do is help him think differently about himself and his situation. You are there to help him reframe his perceptions. Incidents that happened in the past must be confined to the past; the child must be helped to appreciate why the bully might be behaving in the way he does; he must be helped to appreciate that very often the only reason the bully attacks him is because he knows that he will get an entertaining reaction.

Dealing with both the bully and the victim as though they were victims is the clue to success. They both need clear guidelines to establish who is in charge. They both need to know that somebody is interested in their affairs. They both need to perceive themselves differently and to shake off their established image.

CONCLUSION

Aggression may be promoted in a number of ways. In this chapter we have looked at both the positive and negative results of placing children in playgroups and nursery schools. We have considered the importance of play in childhood development and the part that aggression on television might have in promoting aggressive tendencies. We have also examined possible ways in which we can view bullying.

I hope you will have been encouraged to think carefully about these issues in relation to the child who may be at the centre of your concern.

A common factor in all these matters is the issue of intent. If as a parent your intention in placing a child in a playgroup or nursery school is to get him off your hands, then you can guarantee that the plan will backfire on you. He will sense rejection and react accordingly; you will feel guilt and be either aggressive towards him or spoil him. If you have clarified both your needs and his before sending him to playgroup or nursery school, then he will benefit enormously from the opportunities it can offer him. He will benefit most from your greater sense of security.

If as a child care worker or a teacher your intention is to create a play facility which meets his needs and not yours, you will be helping him to grow into independence and to avoid frustration and aggression. If it is your intention to release his aggression through aggressive play you will be disappointed: he will most likely become more aggressive.

If your intention is to allow him to watch unlimited and uncensored television as a way of keeping him passive, you will find that his aggression will intensify. Being passive and overstimulated will lead him to boredom and even more aggression. If you control the use of television it can relieve boredom and act as an appropriate, controlling incentive.

If you see a bully as being someone who intends to harm others then you will find it difficult to see him as a victim. It is necessary to treat both bullies and victims as victims, and to approach them in a controlling and accepting way.

Should your intention be to punish the bully and to shake up the victim you will find that you are promoting the very problem you wish to eliminate.

Examine your intention at all times when you are dealing with an aggressive child. Remember, you can guarantee an aggressive reaction when he perceives injustice, inconsistency and unfairness. If you have thought about your actions and genuinely feel that they are in his interests, reactive episodes of aggression will gradually diminish.

4 Aggressive Adolescents

When an aggressive child reaches his teenage years his aggression appears to intensify. You may often feel extremely threatened by his very presence, for he has now grown to an unmanageable size. In part, though, your apprehension may be caused by the popular conception of the teenage years as a time of instability, when youngsters go through the traumatic developmental process called adolescence. You are expecting him to present problems, almost to the point that you would worry if he did not.

It is worth noting, however, that only ten per cent of the adolescent population actually experiences a personal crisis during the teenage years. Most young people progress to adulthood without noticeable problems and the rate of disturbance for adolescents does not differ significantly from the population at large. You should therefore be wary of accepting the notion that problems are to be expected with teenagers. Your expectations could become self-fulfilling.

One can question the very notion of adolescence as a developmental stage, just as one can question any broad description of human behaviour. We are all different, and when attempting to understand the aggressive adolescent it is worth remembering this. The idea of human beings developing in stages which can accurately explain individual behaviour is useful as an aid to understanding, but you must always bear in mind that every person will deviate in some way from any theoretical model. In Chapter 1 we examined the notion that we are all born with certain qualities, and that we are thereafter subjected to unique circumstances. Not everybody will therefore comply with a developmental pattern.

However, a large school of thought does see adolescence as a distinct phase of development, believing that between the ages of ten and sixteen years there is a surge in the strength of the emotions—with the exception of anger which is already highly developed in childhood. There is also a significant level of disturbance in the way young people see themselves, especially in early adolescence.

Whatever your viewpoint may be on the question of adolescence as a developmental stage, the concept is a good one in that it helps you to begin thinking rather more objectively about the young person who may be causing you so many problems. If you recognise the concept of adolescence, then he will be among the small number of teenagers who are susceptible to its pressures.

If you are to avoid persistent confrontation you must see him as someone who needs help, rather than as an awkward personality who can only be left to cope on his own; as with your approach to bullies, you must see him as a victim of his own vulnerability and circumstances. It is not very easy to do this, since he will usually present a very real physical threat. Success will come if you reframe your opinion of him, if you alter your conception of his position. This will change your approach and could change his behaviour.

IDENTITY FORMATION

A child continually develops towards independence. We have seen in Chapter 2 how he bonds with his mother in the early stages of life and thereafter grows into a separate person. This is a very gradual process. Throughout his life he will retain many of the anchor points established in his early years.

In his move towards separateness he identifies with the family as a whole. He wants to create his identity—to be recognised as an individual—but not at the expense of losing those close to him. During adolescence he is willing to lose certain family ties and to be subjected to a great deal of stress in his quest for independence. The stress experience is necessary as a strengthening process.

We all have a built-in need to create our own identity. This strong desire for independence, a sense of self, is seen as a central characteristic of any human being. It is a master trait, the framework around which we stretch our canvas of personality, enabling us to cope with the world about us. Through our sense of identity, of consistency, we can allay anxiety by filtering observations which are not consistent with this clear frame of reference.

Growing independence means making new attachments; it is a time when one must accept one's own sexuality, a time when one must come to terms with the rules of society and balance these with strong feelings of assertiveness. The quest for identity appears to reach a crisis point in the teenage years but it is a process that carries on throughout life.

THE UNKNOWN

During childhood the rules and regulations governing life are usually quite clear. A child knows where he belongs; he knows who are the significant people in his life. Others are in charge, and his time is structured by them.

In adolescence the boundaries and controls disappear, and at the same time the young adult senses a need to organise time himself if he is to achieve, to make his mark. His life is full of possibilities, but it is also full of uncertainties. He floats between a strong sense of belonging to the children's world and the knowledge that he is not a full member of the adult group. He is in the margins of life.

We therefore see behaviour patterns change during adolescence. As the young adult crystallises his boundaries—creates his own world—we see him bouncing against the old one. He tests its strength and measures his capabilities to survive alone. He begins to make decisions and his position is strengthened as others question his reasoning. He senses his self as he pitches and rolls forward; he experiences proactive movement. He is becoming less helpless and more able to determine his own future.

For the more vulnerable child the natural move towards independence will be extremely difficult. He needs a safe environment and cannot easily cope with change. He relies heavily on consistent rules and on their being applied fairly by someone else. If he bounces against the world it will be in confusion and frustration. He will react with intense episodes of aggression as he feels thwarted in his attempt to assert himself.

THE DILEMMA

Teenagers wish to belong and yet they wish to be separate. They need the recognition and acceptance of society and at the same time they need to assert their individuality. They need a role.

Adolescence is the time when they make meaning of the world in which they are to exist. It can be viewed as a transitional time when they must balance their perception of self with the outside world.

It has also been described as a moratorium. At this time a young adult is deciding whether he should make a complete break with his past and become somebody quite different, or whether he should struggle to integrate his past with his future self. If he decides on the latter course, he will achieve a positive resolution: he will feel at home in his own body, he will sense where he is going and will feel strong ties with significant people in his life. If he chooses to sever his past he will achieve a negative identity. He will not be at ease with himself, he will not know where he is going in life and he will have no stabilising anchor points from the past.

In this respect adolescents can be divided into four groups: those who have reached the crossroads and made a commitment; those who are at the crossroads and have not yet committed themselves; those who have made a commitment without encountering the crossroads; and those whose drive towards the crossroads is diffuse.

During adolescence we therefore see young adults presenting all manner of roles. They experiment in identifying with a variety of models. The bizarre nature of these is as much a reflection of their intense need to belong as to be separate. They struggle through all sorts of crises in relation to dress, manner, relationships and attitudes as they attempt to make some meaningful relationship with their world.

During the deciding time, the moratorium, most young people make some kind of a break with their past and yet retain a lot from it for the future. If they were to make a complete break they would simply not be able to survive; if they made no break at all they would remain locked in childhood. Making the break is therefore essential. It is how the break is made that determines whether the past is lost—and, with it, future security.

For the well balanced child the process can be difficult; for the vulnerable child it can be impossible. He needs to belong, and any transitional period during which he might find himself on his own will result in uncontrolled aggression.

Special attention needs to be given to creating bridging associations: he should be involved in a variety of group settings from an early age. These will provide a network of supportive people to whom he can attach himself as he begins to make his own world. He will depend on someone arranging this: do not rely on him making his own way towards creating his identity. To avoid heightened frustration and aggression during his adolescence you must plan ahead. He will always need to have a strong sense of belonging, and if you do not transfer his attachment he will be dependent on you for the rest of his life. If you can arrange for him to attend a youth group, or take part in some regular group activity, you will be helping him to achieve a sense of identity outside the home.

Because of their behaviour towards others, aggressive children are often kept at home. This tendency should be resisted. If they are to learn how to relate to others and are to assume some kind of personal identity in adolescence, they need to mix as much as possible. Rather than keep them away from everyone during childhood you should spread them around. People, including yourself, can usually tolerate them in small doses, and meaningful relationships can be managed in this way, providing that those who have agreed to take part are fully aware of why they are doing so. During his adolescence it is important for the difficult child to have a variety of attachments from which he can make a choice, and if he has come to know a number of people he will be able to sense where he might belong. If he has a feeling of being trapped, with no choice, he will react with increasingly difficult behaviour.

We shall be discussing the need for recruits in Part Two, Chapter 3.

THE ADOLESCENT

IS

WALKING INTO THE UNKNOWN

FROM

THE KNOWN

THE AGGRESSIVE ADOLESCENT

IS

WALKING INTO THE UNKNOWN

FROM

THE UNACCEPTABLE

THE CHALLENGE

Adolescents are faced with a number of challenges: they must relinquish the values and beliefs they had as young children; they must relive traumas experienced in childhood so that they can master them and not be subjected to them for the rest of their lives; they must accept their personal history (since one cannot have a future without a past); and they must create a firm sense of their sexuality.

When these four challenges are met the result is growth towards full autonomy and stability. This is a gradual process which carries on throughout adulthood.

As they progress towards a synthesis of their past behaviour and their future aspirations, adolescents will exhibit a greater degree of inconsistency. Their beliefs and values will be intense and then may suddenly fade; new values will replace previously declared convictions; these in turn will be refined and adjusted as the young adult begins to fit them into his scheme of things.

There may be regression into childhood mannerisms and behaviour as he finally clears the ground for the new values to take root. He may ask questions about his personal history and an honest response will be demanded, for he needs to be sure of the past before he can move on. He will experiment with relationships, especially with the opposite sex, in an attempt to clarify his sexual status and identity.

The vulnerable child will feel the confusion of this process and be unable to understand the increasing number of unfairnesses that he sees around him; he may react with violent aggression as he relives the traumas of his early life. He may not be able to cope with any different picture of the past that is presented to him and may simply reject it and detach himself. When he asks questions related to his personal history he will be wanting to hear only that everything is as he thought it was—he will not be able to accept anything very different. He will always have found relationships very difficult and when, during adolescence, he begins to feel the strong need to relate to his peers, he will become increasingly frustrated. Because of his incapacity to form relationships he will be unable to sense his sexuality. Problems with female relationships will reinforce this lack of sexual identity.

Aggressive children are unable to meet the challenges of adolescence without assistance.

Outbursts of aggression may be avoided by forethought on your part: think very carefully about the implications of any new situation. Good communication is the clue to much success with the aggressive child, whether it be in relation to actions, scenarios or relationships. If matters can be foreseen and explained beforehand, then what you will have said to him will be accepted as fair when the experience occurs. If something happens for which you have not laid the ground rules, he will have to work it out for himself and may become frustrated.

However, new situations beyond your control will inevitably occur; in any case, he will be quite capable of fabricating motives and scenarios and will do this as a matter of course as he feels the urge to establish his own boundaries. In these instances all you can do is appreciate what is going on. What you must *not* do is become a participant in the game—in other words, you must not become emotionally involved and upset. You must remember that often the game is about whether or not you care for him, and if there is a hint of this you must make it clear to him that you do.

Physical safety, both yours and his, will be your principal concern and you should take the necessary action to prevent harm being done. We shall be discussing techniques to cope with this in Part Two, Chapter 3.

SELF-APPRAISAL

The adolescent is heavily involved in self-appraisal as part of the process towards a sense of identity. He appraises himself in relation to his peers.

His physical appearance is particularly important to him. During adolescence many physiological changes take place, and boys welcome these because they are a sign that they are entering manhood. Those who mature early are more popular, more relaxed and better natured. Late maturers are less adequate and lack self-confidence. They tend to be more anxious since physical maturation confirms sexual identity. The maturational process is not so welcome among girls, since they find that, unlike boys, they remain at the same height while their weight continues to increase.

As hormonal levels alter, both boys and girls suffer the effects of oily skin and have to contend with unattractive pimples and acne. While muscular boys are popular because they are better at sport, fat boys find difficulty in relating to peers, and thin boys tend to be submissive.

When an adolescent thinks of himself he is concerned not only with his body image but with aspects of his personality: he judges himself and his peers on the ability to learn, to think, to reason and to remember; he assesses ability in specific fields such as the arts or mechanics. Performance in sport is very important. Clothes and grooming become items on which he judges himself and others. Attitudes to school are important to him, as is the ability to socialise. He begins to acknowledge personal character traits in himself and others.

The adolescent may identify with any of these qualities. If he feels that in relation to his peers he is equal, then his sense of identity will be positively enhanced; should he fail to measure up to their standards he must have the capacity to accept this. If he cannot, then his behaviour will alter considerably as his defence mechanisms (Chapter 1) come into play. He will assume a negative identity and a negative approach to life.

Vulnerable children have reached a negative state of identity well before their adolescence. They are unable to make relationships with their peers other than on a negative basis as they begin to defend themselves at a very early age. During the time of their adolescence they have an increased awareness of the gap between all aspects of their performance and those of their peers. The comparison of attributes so necessary for the creation of a sense of identity has already established a truly negative effect on them. It is at this time, however, that they come to realise it.

There is really only one effective solution, and it is a long term one: we must from the very beginning ensure that we project to all children that, rather than being the same as others, we should appreciate our differences; that we are not here to compete with others so much as to help them and to improve our own performance.

The more vulnerable a child is the more likely he will be to model himself on others. If you as a parent, child care worker or teacher adopt a truly caring attitude you will embody within it an appreciation of everyone's differences. The vulnerable child in particular will always need this approach on which to model himself.

You will constantly need to remember the importance of creating a positive self-image for him. Despite the difficulties he presents to you, you must reinforce his good points not only by praising him when they arise, but by referring to positive image-makers whenever possible. In other words, you should take every opportunity to refer to scenarios in the past when he displayed a particularly attractive quality. You should quite deliberately calculate the kind of image you would like him to have and think of ways in which you could help him to assume it.

There is nothing to fear from this, either in practical or ethical terms. The vulnerable, aggressive child has a very weak image of himself: this, in essence, is his vulnerability. He reacts aggressively to defend a self which has failed to crystallise. Should you take no action to try and create a self-image for him his condition will deteriorate, especially as he approaches adolescence. This is a time when self-appraisal intensifies. You will know when your projected self-image for him will work. If it does not, then try something else. A guiding principle is that you should try to think the way he does and choose something which would have immediate appeal.

We will be returning to practical techniques with more precise suggestions in Part Two, Chapter 2.

THE GENERATION GAP

Adolescence is a time of increased tension between parents and their offspring, when adults usually begin to make greater demands on children in terms of performance. The idealism of young people is often seen by adults as a lack of realism, and the generation gap is intensified by an intrinsic physical difference: adults envy the young for their physical prowess, and the young resent adults for the condition of the world in which they find themselves.

The degree of tension between the generations at this time is related to the path an adolescent may have taken when or if he reached the crossroads (see p. 59). He may have decided to reject his past and make a complete break because of the tension arising between him and his parents. He may prevaricate endlessly, unable to make a decision and creating an interminable relationship based on stress. He may, on the other hand, have made a commitment one way or the other without much fuss; or his drive towards the crossroads may be so weak and diffuse that he appears ineffectual and apathetic.

The tendency is for adults to criticise him heavily for taking any of these courses of action, despite the fact that they are beyond his conscious control. They resent it if he rejects his past, including them and the way they have raised him; they cannot appreciate it when he is unable to resolve issues and when he is ambivalent about everything—the resulting stress is too much to take. They worry about him if he sails along with no sign of a protest—but they worry even more about themselves and tend to think that they have raised a conformist, a wimp. When he is nowhere near approaching the crossroads they reject him because he is so weak and compliant; they feel guilty about having raised such an ineffectual person for whom they might still be responsible in his adulthood.

The aggressive, difficult child is rejected by most adults, and in adolescence he will be rejected even further as responsibility for him becomes unbearable. Since babyhood he has reacted particularly badly to any form of criticism; when this intensifies during adolescence, the second phase of separation, the tension often results in forced physical separation from his past. He will assault someone and be taken away, or desert as a means of personal survival.

The aggressive child who turns his aggression inwards and is liable to self-mutilate will be at the extremes of his condition during this period. He may attempt suicide in an effort to resolve the situation: this may be his way of making a commitment. He may retreat into a psychotic condition in which his world becomes tolerable.

A great deal of tension could be allayed if parents and those caring for young adults appreciated the suggested processes which are seen as the elements of adolescence. A good starting point is to realise that whenever we act we do so in the role of a child, an adult or a parent. Very often it is assumed that children should behave like adults; they are expected somehow to be at the same stage of development. Yet often adults will behave like children and fail to see that they are doing so.

Adults will unconsciously assume the role of a parent when they are talking to a young adult—an adolescent—and treat him like a child, but adolescents should be respected for what they are: adults who are just beginning to learn the ropes and are making a lot of necessary mistakes.

Parents and carers should therefore reappraise their own position. They should regard themselves as responsible adults, who are capable of seeing children as children and young adults as young adults. They should appreciate the need for a generation gap and the part they play in it. They are there to provide a constant, fixed platform from which the next generation can take off. If they are to help the more vulnerable young adult assume his flight path they must prepare for the inevitably stormy weather ahead. Understanding what a young adult may be feeling as he makes his way towards independence can play a large part in this.

FREEDOMS

Part of an adult's understanding should be to acknowledge the freedom to which the adolescent is aspiring:
1 He is reaching for the freedom to be himself. All of his life he has been guided and controlled by adults; now he wishes to be in charge, to determine his own destiny.
2 He is reaching for the freedom to think—to be independent and creative in his thought processes. He no longer wishes to accept someone else's values.
3 He wants the freedom to pray or not to pray. He wants to be able to love: to be able to retreat when necessary. He wants to determine when he will play and when he will work.

Should these basic needs not be met, then an adolescent's behaviour is likely to become hostile and aggressive—all the more so if he has been aggressive from an early age. His situation is exacerbated by the fact that he will be finding it difficult anyway to negotiate the separation process, simply because he is unable to manage himself without a high degree of external control.

Freedom for the vulnerable child can be life-threatening and he will react defensively when faced with the prospect. He wants the freedoms but at the same time he wants the security of what he has had around him throughout his life. The dilemma results in ambiguous behaviour. The solution readily available for him is blind, seemingly unprovoked, aggression.

The vulnerable child should therefore be given opportunities to experience freedom and decision-making from an early age. It must always be recognised, however, that his primary need is for external control. Any degree of freedom could jeopardise his sense of security and result in episodes of self-reinforcing aggressive behaviour. The times when he is allowed freedom and choice should be gauged very carefully in relation to this. You will be able to tell how secure he is by the way he is able to cope with the freedoms you feel you can allow. Be aware, however, when determining what freedom you can allow him, of your own need for security, and ask yourself whose interests are coming first.

ANGER AND ALIENATION

We saw in Chapter 1 that there are three main reasons why children become angry: firstly, if they are thwarted in achieving their objectives; secondly, when they feel that they are being criticised in any way; and thirdly, when they perceive a situation to be unfair or when rules are not applied consistently.

During adolescence these triggers become even more sensitive. Adolescents are fiercely trying to determine what they wish to achieve. Their achievements will form part of their identity and should they be frustrated by anyone in their attempts, they will react with aggression.

They are particularly angry when they encounter hypocrisy, insincerity, inconsideration, intolerance and dishonesty, and may direct angry aggression to anyone involved in such situations. When they perceive others as being offensive to them in this respect they will see their anger as being entirely justified and will believe that it is not only acceptable for them to retaliate but that it is their duty to do so.

Often they will treat others as they feel they themselves have been treated. They are intolerant of their own limitations and are equally intolerant of failings in others. They have a great deal of personal pride and will regard any threat to this seriously. Placing them in situations, especially public ones, where they will be under an inappropriate degree of pressure from their peers can lead to a serious loss of self-esteem. Interestingly, few adolescents react with physical aggression: verbal protests, avoidance and fantasy are much more common reactions.

It is those who withdraw into their private worlds who cause deep concern. They are alienated from the real world. They feel extremely lonely and unable to achieve any degree of intimacy with those around them. They are without roots and have no sense of purpose. They have a diffuse sense of who they are. Their behaviour is characterised by total egocentricity, distrust and pessimism. They are anxious and feel powerless. They sense a lack of attachment to society.

These extreme symptoms arise when change occurs too frequently for the adolescent to integrate the past with the present, when he is experiencing gross uncertainties in his life. They are promoted by his desire to be successful, especially in material and financial terms, and by the pressure often exerted upon him to adopt traditional values—to conform. A common scenario for all these factors is a setting which promotes a macho image and which appears as uncaring.

Alienated young people appear in the guise of escapists who continue to live in their childhood world, a small number of reformers who fight against all value systems, or anti-social youths who, as radical protestors, flout the law and drift into delinquency. Alienation can be considered a necessary element of adolescence, part of this second phase of separation, but as with everything else in life, it is a matter of concern when its intensity is self-destructive. It should be an enriching and enabling process in which growth takes place.

We can see that for the vulnerable aggressive child the period of his adolescence can be particularly traumatic. He will need an enormous amount of support and sympathetic understanding if he is to survive this transitional period. He is more likely than most to become angry and alienated.

CONCLUSION

It is important to stress that alienation and rejection are quite rare. The majority of adolescents experience no significant trauma as they progress through their teenage years; the processes we have examined are taken in their stride and throughout their lives they continue to share values and beliefs with their parents, enjoying harmonious relationships with them and looking to them for approval and support. Whereas peers may play a larger part in helping them with current situational dilemmas, parents are used to guide them in decision-making for the long-term future. The home and family remain with them as their psychological platform and the more secure this base, the more they will be able to glide through their developmental processes, not just during adolescence but to full maturation.

The educational process plays a large part in determining whether or not they experience difficulty. Adolescence begins almost at the same time that children experience a change in their pattern of schooling. They move to a less secure educational setting with frequent class changes and are required to be more independent. Competitive examinations create a great deal of stress at a time when physiological changes might be thought to be enough. Those who go on to higher education may resent the necessary dependency on parents; those who leave school and are unemployed suffer from a significant increase in distress and morbidity.

Both the home and the school can help the adolescent to avoid rejecting them. They can help him retain the security of his past by making family and school life a strong and meaningful part of his self, something which he wants to keep.

Vulnerable, aggressive children, more than others, need

this strong sense of security, of belonging and of external control. They need to know where they will always belong before they can begin to become independent. They have a distorted perception of the world around them and need somebody to clarify their objectives, to protect them from unthinking criticism and to provide a clear framework of fair and consistent rules. If there is no one to do this they will in their frustration react with angry aggression.

For all young people adolescence is a time of strong feelings and severe mood swings. The reactions of aggressive children can in adolescence turn into uncontrolled physical violence, unless there is somebody who understands what they may be experiencing. Should you be that person, the hope is that, having absorbed the issues in this chapter, you will be able sensibly to devise some appropriate strategies for dealing with the very difficult young person you have at the centre of your concern.

5 Families

We have seen that there are two central, interdependent factors that may make a child behave aggressively: his emotional condition and his life experience. A child is born with his own emotional characteristics. He may be vulnerable or resilient. Thereafter he has to cope with the circumstances in which he finds himself. If he is a vulnerable child his behaviour may cause a great deal of difficulty for others as he struggles to create and maintain a sense of personal identity; if he is resilient he will take life in his stride and present few problems. He will know who he is in relation to his past, and he will have a clear picture of where he is going.

The more vulnerable a child is the more he will need a supportive environment. Should there be a mismatch between his needs and what is available for him, then he will become more vulnerable; every time his needs are met he will become more resilient.

A commonly held belief is that a primary need of every child is to exist in what has been described as a nuclear family: a setting where there is a mother and a father and their children. This is the setting which is thought to promote optimum development. When we are considering the needs of aggressive children, however, we may question this since it is in the family setting that people are most likely to suffer from violence.

Most people who restrain their emotions in other social settings feel able to unleash them within the confines of the home. They can do this and still maintain their social respectability. Those outside the family will continue to acknowledge them as reasonable, self-controlled people with whom they can feel safe and on whom they can rely. Society demands consistency, rather than the emotional peaks and troughs which we all experience.

Violence in families would seem to be almost endemic. Wife beating has always taken place: in Roman times it was seen as a marital right. Anthropologists have accepted that when people began to live together in small units and surround themselves with walls, they began to hit each other.

Child abuse is one of the most common causes of death among pre-school children in the United Kingdom; hundreds of children die each year as a result of maltreatment by their parents. Battering parents come from all social classes and are most common in families where the mother is between 20 and 30 years old. Battering fathers are usually around 26 years old and have a history of unemployment or illness. They often have criminal records for other offences.

Children also suffer at the hands of their brothers and sisters; 80 per cent of children between the ages of three and seventeen are involved in at least one annual incident of violent conflict with their siblings. One teenager in ten makes a violent attack annually on his parents; three per cent of these attacks could be regarded as serious physical assault.

A degree of violent interaction in families may be a necessary and valuable experience for most children, but for the vulnerable child it can only worsen his condition. He needs the security of a fixed pattern of relationships and cannot cope with family conflict or instability. He is unstable within himself.

We should question whether any family setting is the best place for an emotionally fragile child. Our immediate instinct is to say that the family is the one place where he could be given the warmth and affection which he needs if he is to feel secure. However, the situation is more complex than this.

It is easier for all of us to relate well to people who are in a non-affective role; when we have to interact with those who are close to us we can find it much more difficult. This applies especially when we are intrinsically fragile. For the vulnerable child the family may present more problems than support. Everything might be too close for him to handle. He is disabled in terms of coping with his feelings and family dynamics might prove too much for him.

Whether you are a parent, a child care worker or a teacher, you must be aware of the inherent stresses which the family setting promotes. For the resilient person it can easily provide a safe environment in which feelings can be expressed and relationships tested. Personal growth can take place without risk. For the vulnerable person it can be a setting where, in the absence of careful planning by mindful parents, personal frustrations are exaggerated and expressed in uncontrolled aggression.

In many families where there is a disturbed and aggressive child, there is a high level of violent interaction between family members. When we come to discuss how we might help the aggressive child, in Part Two, we shall see how, by withdrawing him from the family setting, we can give him the opportunity to operate in an environment which makes fewer affective demands on him, and how at the same time we can give other members of the family a chance to experience a more positive way of interacting with each other. Too often we assume that the child needs to be with his family; a great deal of abuse could be avoided if more recognition were given to the fact that some children are born with an inability to relate to others on an affective level.

UNDERSTANDING THE PARENTS

If we wish to diminish aggression in a child we should appreciate that both children and adults can be vulnerable. The situation is complex: the family is essentially a sophisticated set of interactions, which tends to escalate any element of aggression or other emotion within its dynamics. No one member is to blame. Because of our feeling of helplessness, we have a tendency when faced with situations which threaten us to look for a scapegoat: parents blame their children and care workers blame the parents. Blaming others is a sign of ignorance and weakness, however. If we can examine a family problem without feeling the need for retribution, we shall be looking in the right direction for a solution.

When we think of violence occurring in families, we tend to have a picture in our mind of wives or children being physically beaten, usually by the husband or father. We lay the blame at his door. The truth is that all members of a family play a part in episodes of domestic violence. Both fathers and mothers batter their children, and children themselves play a less than passive part in the proceedings.

If an adult is abusing either a partner or a child it is likely that he or she is also a victim of abuse. This abuse may have been physical or emotional and have occurred during childhood. He or she is likely to have experienced some form of institutional care or severe disruption in the family. On the other hand, it may be actual or perceived abuse which is taking place in the present.

As discussed on p. 73, much abuse on children is inflicted by men and women in their early twenties. This is a time when many have just begun to live independently, away from their own family. They may be in the first stages of learning to live with a new person, and finding that they have committed themselves to an unrealistic partnership. A child may be a responsibility which they feel they cannot meet either materially or emotionally. Their loss of personal freedom may be deeply resented; teenage dreams and aspirations may be completely broken. They may perceive their personal situation to be unjust; they may feel a sense of helplessness. They may *feel* that they are being abused.

In their frustration they may become aggressive, inflict violence on others, or withdraw from the world around them. A child often becomes the target for their aggression, especially when it is a child who demands a great deal of attention. Children who are sickly and continually cry often provoke abuse, particularly from parents who, because of their own fragility, may already be under a great deal of stress. The child might be physically assaulted, emotionally rejected or both.

Abusing parents may present as depressed and passive personalities; they may be emotionally cold and make unrealistic and excessive demands on children. They may, on the other hand, be habitually aggressive and prone to outbursts of temper in the home. Their aggression in one form or another is released against the source of their irritation.

Parents who abuse children know that they are doing something wrong; their guilt aggravates the situation. They become increasingly frustrated and even more aggressive. Their aggression, particularly when directed towards children, alienates them from their community and their sense of isolation, which is often a central cause for the release of uncontrolled emotions, is intensified. They feel that there is no one to turn to; they are incompetent, helpless and at the mercy of their emotions. They are abusers who feel abused.

All children present parents with additional stress, but the emotionally fragile child can easily take a young mother or father to breaking point. Mothers, whose emotions may be particularly finely tuned following the birth of their child, might easily be tempted to smother the cause of their intense irritation in a seemingly inexplicable course of action. Young fathers, working with the uncertainty of employment and tired from sleepless nights, might lash out at a screaming infant in confusion and desperation. When a child is abused it should not be presumed that he is completely innocent; a fragile child may irritate even the most resilient of mature adults.

Whatever the causes may be for children being abused, we know that if they are abused they are likely to become abusers themselves. If we are to prevent this happening it is important to examine the needs of parents, not just children. We must think of abusing parents as they think of themselves—as being abused. We shall then be able to give them the support they need.

Parents need to be listened to in order that they may be strengthened. If they know that someone is aware of how they see their situation, this may be enough for them to feel strong enough to take some form of action. They do not need anyone to tell them that they are getting things wrong; as we have said already, they know this. Most anger and aggression expressed by parents is the result of perceived failure. At the forefront is their frustration at not being able to achieve material success. In our society, if they have nothing they are nothing. Sickness and unemployment compound the problem, promoting a negative sense of identity which can be visited on their children.

If parents of aggressive children are given support, the aggression of their children rapidly diminishes.

THE SINS OF THE FATHERS

Parents of aggressive children have often experienced difficulties during their own childhood. They may have grown

HELP

THE

PARENT

AND YOU WILL

HELP

THE CHILD

up in a very unhappy atmosphere where their family was continually disrupted. They may have had a teenage mother who was unable to provide proper care; their mother may have been one of the many who stay at home all day looking after at least one child, with nobody to share the parenting. They may have been raised without a father who could give the affection and support a mother needs if she is going to be able to give guidelines and controls to her children.

The parent may have been a fragile child, emotionally vulnerable. She may not have been able to fulfil her intellectual potential because of her vulnerability; she may always have lived on her emotions and been incapable of sustaining relationships.

CRIMINALITY

The parent may have come from a family in which one or more of the members was a criminal. Children who have criminal parents have a much greater tendency to be delinquent, especially when the parent is criminally active during the early period of child-rearing.

Children who have delinquent brothers and sisters are also at a greater degree of risk in relation to deviant behaviour. This is not to imply that there is a significant genetic basis for criminality. Other dominant characteristics of such families are thought to play a much larger part in the development of disturbed, anti-social behaviour: persistent unemployment, alcoholism and abnormal parental personality traits are associated with criminality. The risk of a child becoming delinquent is found to be greatest in a family setting where there is an absence of care and discipline, where the family relationships are disturbed and where there is a cruel and neglectful criminal father.

It is easy to see how a vulnerable child could become disturbed in such a family setting. Although we should not equate disturbance with delinquency, it is clear that the fragile personality could only survive in such circumstances by modelling on his family patterns of behaviour. Fragile children will quickly grasp at powerful models around them in their search for an identity.

Vulnerable children find it difficult to form relationships:

if they begin to steal it is thought that they may be replacing missing relationships with possessions. Children who feel unloved and who have been over-controlled are those most likely to steal. They have been dominated to the degree where they do not have the opportunity to test out their parents; they steal, and lie about it. When they receive a strong response their stealing and lying is reinforced. Stealing usually occurs when there is tenuous attachment between the child and the parent, and when the parent himself tends towards delinquency.

Children who steal or set fire to things, who destroy property and commit acts of vandalism, often come from homes where there is a high degree of violence. They have often witnessed adult sexual behaviour.

MENTAL ILLNESS

While it is generally accepted that schizophrenia and major depressive disorders may have a genetic origin, the effect of any kind of parental personality disorder on a child cannot be denied.

Parental mental disorders can lead to gross marital discord. Parents will conflict over child-rearing practices; there may be little consistency regarding the pattern of dominance in the family; a parent may not be able to relate to a partner; a child might be resented and rejected.

Mental disorders can have a contagious effect. One parent may, over a period of time, infect the other with a distorted perception of the world; the couple may become socially isolated. Children in the family will suffer because of the detachment from society and an inability to perceive the world in other than negative, threatening terms.

Mental illness may involve the hospitalisation of the parent; it may mean the removal of the child from the family home. In either instance the vulnerable child will be affected by the separation.

Any kind of health problem may make a parent irritable, aggressive and hostile. If a child has been brought up in a home where the parent has suffered a long-term illness, he will have experienced the harsh reality of human existence before his time.

However, although we must recognise that parental mental disorder presents a risk to children, it must never be concluded that all children will be adversely affected by their parent's illness. The greatest risk occurs where there is gross family discord, where both parents are ill to the point that they are unable to function effectively as parents, and where their behaviour directly impinges on the life of the child. The children most likely to be affected by such conditions will of course be those who are emotionally vulnerable.

FAMILY SIZE

Neither the parent nor the child decides the size of the family into which he is born, or the ordinal position in which he finds himself. Children from large families have a lower level of verbal intelligence and reading attainment, possibly because there is less intensive interaction and less opportunity for the development of effective communication skills than there is in small families, and because less encouragement is given for academic attainment. They may suffer from overcrowding and material hardship: parental discord and conflict is often rooted here. The level of parental control and the quality of discipline can be jeopardised in such circumstances. Accordingly children from large families are more restless, disobedient and destructive. They tend to bully and fight more than children who come from small families.

On the other hand, children from small families can suffer from over-indulgence by the parent. An only child is often regarded as precious. He may have been born under difficult circumstances after a period of sterility, a series of miscarriages or deaths of other children. It could be said that he is over-valued and therefore over-protected. A parent will have excessive contact with him; she will mother him for too long, excluding all other relationships; she will prolong the process of infantile care, bathing and feeding him and generally being at his beck and call; she will prevent any move towards independence by not allowing him to help around the house, and by trying to fight all his battles for him. In many instances she is emotionally dependent on the child, and if she was raised in a home lacking warmth and love she may be determined to give her child all the love she missed. If she has no social life with her partner she may compensate by investing emotionally in the child, recognising the futility of her marital relationship.

The effect on the child is to increase the level of his disturbance. He should be growing towards independence, assuming a sense of identity, of separateness. The parent needs him more than he needs the parent. The more he is smothered the more he will react with aggressive outbursts or fade into a fantasy world.

POSITION IN THE FAMILY

The first-born in a family is likely to be a higher achiever, both scholastically and at work, than those born later; the last-born is particularly prone to scholastic failure. The first-born is, however, more likely to develop an emotional disorder. While he may receive more love and attention than his siblings, his parents are likely to be more anxious, pressurising and controlling than they are with later children. The eldest child has also to adjust to the arrival of the others. Often there will be a regression in his toilet training on the birth of a new baby; the problem is usually transient, but regression may persist in this and other ways, especially if the parent punishes the child for his naughty behaviour. A hostile relationship often exists between siblings when there has been an intense and warm interaction between the parent and the first child; a rather more detached relationship between the parent and the first-born will result in an amicable interaction between the two children.

The arrival of the second child always changes the dynamics within the family. Whether or not any of the members will be adversely affected depends on too many factors to enable one to be precise about the long-term effects on a child. We must be aware, however, of the central part that a child's intrinsic vulnerability may play in this matter. If a child is not very resilient within himself he may react extremely badly to the arrival of another child; if he is the new arrival he may be badly affected by the hostile reception he receives from his sibling.

Whether a child comes from a large family or a small one and whether he is the first or last child in the family does not necessarily mean that he will be disturbed. The family is a phenomenon in which there is a great interplay of variables. The size of the family and the ordinal position of a child within it are two of these. Each child will react differently to his family circumstances according to the strength of those around him and his own level of resilience.

SIGNIFICANT PEOPLE

Disturbed, aggressive children often come from families where the lines of communication and authority are blurred. When members discuss matters they do so in a negative fashion and no clear decisions are ever reached. This may be because there is no one person in the family who is strong enough to take responsibility.

In normal families there is no fixed pattern of dominance which could be said to create disturbance in children. Fathers make decisions and mothers make decisions. Some decisions are made conjointly. Problems arise when conflicting messages are given by a parent—when, for example, a mother by her facial expression gives one message and by her voice another. Problems also arise, especially for the less resilient child, when because of parental discord there is no firm agreement on anything. Vulnerable children need to have a clear picture of family relationships. Ambivalent feelings between parents will only add to their problems. Far better for the child if the warring parents were to separate.

Other complications for the child might be caused by grandparents who live too close to the family. While the family with a problem child needs to recruit the help of others (see Part Two, Chapter 3), it is often a fatal mistake to involve close family members.

Grandparents in particular often seem to over-involve themselves with their grandchild when he is in some way disabled. Their intentions are always honourable, but the effect of their intrusion can be disastrous. A child who is experiencing no difficulties is usually spoilt by his grandparents; the fragile child can be damaged beyond repair. Grandparents are removed from the realities of daily life when it comes to looking after an aggressive child who may be manipulative and self-centred and quite capable of behaving well for the short time that his grandparents are available to spoil him.

Grandparents can transmit conflicting messages to the child; often the essence of the problem is that they tend to make decisions for the parents, and the child becomes confused over who is in charge. This happens to its worst effect when the grandparents are living almost on the family doorstep.

As we have already stated, the grandparents are not the only participants in this scenario. We have them and the manipulative child acting their respective parts—and of course the parents, who have most likely relinquished control out of sheer exhaustion.

The vulnerable child needs some significant people in his life outside the home and the extended family. Such people as youth leaders can provide an escape valve for him. He will often model himself on them and refer to them for general guidelines regarding his behaviour. He will more readily listen to them than to his parents, since because of their emotional distance they can give him clear and unequivocal signals.

DISCIPLINE

Discipline is important for all children since it implies that there are boundaries for behaviour, a shape to existence. For the vulnerable child it is the breath of life, enabling him to grow within its safety towards his own personal control system.

Parents tend to impose their own experience of discipline on their child and it is perhaps significant that those with problem children exert few controls. Children in these families spend a great deal of time out of sight of their parents; their behaviour is not monitored and controlled. Their parents often do not know where they are or what they are doing. Children with conduct problems see their parents as unable to set limits to their behaviour. They receive no explicit guidance on how to behave and their parents tend to avoid any matters which might lead to confrontation. When problems do arise the parents may shout and gesticulate, but fail to follow the matter through with sanctions.

This style of discipline transmits a message of rejection to the child and is ineffective because it is a reflection of the parent's mood rather than the child's behaviour.

Discipline involves arriving at solutions to problems and, as we have seen above, families with difficult children are usually unable to arrive at decisions. Any discipline tends therefore to be both negative and diffuse. Children will only comply with the requests of adults whom they respect. Discipline is achieved in families which have shared positive experiences, but in families with problem children these are sadly lacking.

We all recognise that children need discipline. The hard part is the practical implementation.

If we control too heavily and refuse to listen to anything the child may say, we promote a lack of conscience, low self-esteem and social withdrawal. We may even promote such problems as stealing and lying (see p. 79).

If we are indulgent or permissive we promote a lack of impulse control in the child and suffer from his aggressive outbursts.

If we are indifferent to the child's behaviour and take no notice of it we are again promoting aggression, low self-esteem and low levels of personal control.

If, however, we are able to combine firm and clear rule-setting with a pleasant form of interaction with the child, we shall promote a sense of responsibility within him and diminish his tendency towards aggression. Feeling that he has an important part to play in any decision-making, his self-esteem will be enhanced and he will become more independent. It is a good idea always to be one step ahead of a child; in this way damaging episodes of confrontation can be avoided. We shall be discussing preventative techniques in Part Two.

MEETING PARENTS

Understanding why parents might experience problems when raising difficult children is important, but we also need

DISCIPLINE

IS THE BREATH OF

LIFE

BUT ONLY WHEN

IT IS ACCOMPANIED BY

ENJOYABLE

SHARED

EXPERIENCES

to be prepared for the way in which they might present themselves.

Parents of difficult children, and especially those children who cause problems in the neighbourhood because of their aggression, often feel very guilty. They feel as though they are entirely responsible for the behaviour of the child. Their problem would not be so terrible if their child were physically disabled or intellectually impaired, but because he looks physically well and is not mentally disabled it is thought by society that he is somehow evil. The implication is that nothing can be done. This obviously hurts the parent a great deal. When a child is born the parent invests heavily in him; he is in a way a guarantee of immortality.

A parent will protect herself with defence mechanisms in order to maintain some viability as a person. She may appear brusque or indifferent and uncaring. She may act aggressively, especially towards those in authority: she will be looking for someone to blame for her misfortune. In her helplessness she is searching for someone to take responsibility. Teachers and care workers will be presumed to have the answers to her problems, and someone will need to do something about them.

As we saw in Chapter 2, she will often deny that there is a problem with the child; if she admits to it she may attach a label to the condition, giving it an air of medical respectability. Parents with difficult children often say that the child's behaviour is caused by dyslexia, and that because he couldn't read teachers would either ignore or reprimand him. It was only then that he began to misbehave and become aggressive. This may have been the case, but the fact that learning blocks are created by anxiety—emotional fragility—is rarely recognised since it is somehow thought to be a worse reflection on parents themselves. Many difficult children have dyslexia, allergies and phobias which disappear overnight when the child is separated from the parent.

The parent may need the labels, but only in the absence of a listening ear. When faced with the parent of an aggressive child, professionals must be aware of the stress under which she is living. An immediate reaction—almost a natural impulse—is to reject her, but this would be wrong. If we are to help the child we must recognise that the first thing to do is to understand and care for the parent.

Parents will often resent the success that an outsider can have with a difficult child. As mentioned above, someone who has no family ties with the child will provide a cleaner emotional relationship to which the vulnerable child will automatically respond, but if no priority is given to supporting the parent then any success with the child will inevitably be short-lived. Parents should recognise their need for help, and professionals should see helping the parent as the first move towards success with the child.

CONCLUSION

The vulnerable child will find it difficult to cope with the emotional demands his family may make on him and yet he needs some form of sheltered environment in which he can feel safe. His family environment should provide consistency in routines and clearly defined rules and regulations; decisions, whether taken separately by each parent or conjointly, should not result in discord and conflict. Family members should enjoy shared experiences, for these will form the bedrock of discipline and control.

Violence occurs more frequently in families than elsewhere and most of it is not reported: children are loyal to their parents despite the abuse they may have experienced. We must never think that the family is automatically the best place for a child to be: fragile children in particular may be at great risk from its tendency to promote violence.

In attempting to understand aggressive children we must recognise that they come from homes where there are other people who all have their stories to tell. If violence takes place in our society this is where it happens—in the complex emotional interactions of the family.

Parents need to be understood if we are to help their children. When they know that there is someone to whom they can turn they feel stronger and more able to control their offspring, and the aggression in the children quickly diminishes. Parenting styles are learnt from childhood. If we understand how a parent was raised we may be able to understand why her child is acting aggressively. We can then alleviate the situation by introducing her to some alternative parenting techniques.

We must not, however, presume that it is only the child's environment that makes him aggressive. Parents in particular should acknowledge that although they may have given birth to the child they are not responsible for the precise nature of this unique human being; if they have other children they will know that they all react differently to the inevitable stresses of family life. Whatever their style of parenting, they have to contend with the unique chemistry of each of their children, all of whom arrive in the melting pot at different times. How the children react will depend on factors too fluid to analyse. We can be certain of only one thing: that even when they are physically alike, have a similar intellectual capacity and experience of life, their achievements and behaviour may differ considerably according to their emotional resilience.

6 Final Considerations

I hope that the first part of this book has raised some questions in your mind and that you have already begun to formulate your own plan of action. It is essential for you to do this, since the techniques I suggest will not necessarily be the most appropriate for the child in your care. Once you have thoroughly absorbed some of the underlying ideas that I have presented, you will then be able subtly to adapt some of the practical methods outlined in Part Two. When you are dealing with children you are dealing with so many variables that any rigid adherence to suggested approaches will stand a good chance of failing. The important thing is to create within yourself a secure platform of operations. In the heat of the moment, when you have to deal with the aggressive child, you will be relying on some broad principles which you have understood. adjusted to suit your own style, temperament and ability, and absorbed into your philosophical stance. Without this preparation, you will only succeed in provoking further aggressive reactions from your child.

If you have read Part One you will have begun to look at the concept of aggression and in doing so will have begun to detach yourself from the child's emotional turmoil. You must begin to see aggression as a phenomenon which you can control, and a first step towards this is to try and understand what it is.

In this part of the book we have questioned whether aggressive children are born this way, or whether they become aggressive because of their life experience. Your conclusion on this would form the cornerstone of any approach you might take towards them.

We also examined the way in which we all employ defence mechanisms to protect ourselves. Do you see aggressive children as being defensive, and what do you think they are defending? Your answers to these questions will also determine your general attitude to an aggressive child.

We saw that when children become angry they do so because they are thwarted in their aims, when someone has criticised them or their friends, or when they perceive a situation to be unjust. Do you agree that to avoid angry reactions it is simply a matter of helping children to achieve their objectives, of ensuring that they and their friends are not criticised, and of being consistent in your application of agreed rules?

It was suggested that children will present difficult behaviour if their basic needs are not met. They need to have a clear picture of the world, an objective in life, a sense of belonging and rootedness, stimulation and love. Without all these they may become aggressive. Do you see the meeting of these needs as forming the basis for your plan of action?

Have you decided how you feel about your aggressive child playing war games or watching violent scenes on television? How do you explain his bullying: do you see him as one of life's victims?

Do you appreciate that the difficulties being experienced by the aggressive adolescent child may all be related to his search for a sense of separateness, for his own identity?

Do you appreciate the level of violence that can occur within the privacy of a family home? Do you feel that children should remain with their families despite the fact that they may not be able to cope with them on an emotional level? Do you see the child happily existing in the family setting as a realistic objective?

You must be clear about where you stand on these issues. It is essential to realise that from an early age a child is capable of interpreting your intent; a fragile child is particularly sensitive to your motives. If you have sorted yourself out on these matters, then it will be clear to the child that you are determined to help him: your approach will have assumed an air of consistency because of the strength of your underlying objectives.

In this final chapter of preparation I would like to lay before you three concepts which form the bedrock of my approach to dealing with difficult, aggressive children. These concepts have already begun to thread their way through

Part One and will be the basis for all that is suggested in Part Two.

EMOTIONAL FRAGILITY

At birth human beings are endowed with varying degrees of intelligence. There is also a wide range in their physical attributes.

We should recognise that people are also born with an emotional quotient. This is not a commonly accepted idea and yet there clearly is this important factor which can affect all human behaviour and performance.

It is not a difficult notion to accept: we all know what it is to feel 'emotionally drained', especially those of us who deal with difficult children, and we all know how our performance can be raised considerably when we have been emotionally charged by some good news. As we go through our lives we strive to reach some degree of consistency, some kind of emotional equilibrium, which can keep us going. Our days are assessed in terms of our emotional state. If we have had a good day it means that we feel good about it; usually it means that we feel good about ourselves.

In many families there may be a child who has a level of intelligence and physical prowess similar to his siblings. He may be expected to have the same capacity to cope with life experiences but this is not the case. After acknowledging that his intellectual and physical abilities will create a unique chemistry, and that his life experiences will be different in many subtle respects, it is clear from the quality of his reactions that the base for his emotional state is different. His brothers and sisters may be able to cope with life; he will find it very difficult.

He is a fragile child who is emotionally vulnerable.

You may say that the aggressive child you are hoping to help is in no way fragile. He may appear exactly the opposite—as a tough, uncaring lout. He may attack you verbally or physically and pay no attention to what you say.

He is doing all of this to protect his fragile self. The more fragile he is the more aggressive he will be. If he were strong within himself he would have no need to act aggressively.

Children who are vulnerable have a high degree of

anxiety. They want situations always to remain the same in order that they can feel secure. They are supersensitive and will react with all the defence mechanisms we mentioned in Chapter 1. They are defending something which is very weak, and sometimes non-existent: they are protecting their sense of identity. If they lose this they will become insane. Their defence mechanisms are therefore employed in full strength and they will exhibit behaviour which may be either overtly aggressive or turned in on themselves.

As I have said, our intellectual and physical performance is affected by our emotional state. The three factors interact and influence each other. If we can put our intellectual or physical abilities to good use then we can enhance our emotional state. However, if our emotional platform—the emotional bottom line—tends towards vulnerability, this process is denied us and we see ourselves as failures.

Many children have innate high intellectual ability and are unable to reach their potential; many have physical attributes which would equip them to be Olympic athletes. They fail because their starting point is different and because nobody recognises the importance of their *emotional quotient*. A sense of failure and frustration leads to either despair or angry aggression.

Emotionally fragile children are disabled in their capacity to relate to other people. They have most difficulty in coping with those closest to them. Family members, and mothers in particular, cause them the greatest problems. We all experience the phenomenon of thinking a great deal of our relatives but preferring them to live at a distance. This is not exactly what I am talking about, but it is closely connected. Fragile people create their own worlds, and there is a great difference between these and the real world around them. This is because of their need to secure for themselves a non-threatening, safe environment. Living with the harsh realities of the family where, as we saw in Chapter 5, people expose emotions, can be too much for them. It is important to accept the notion that the aggressive child is disabled emotionally: he is fragile and vulnerable. To place him in situations which demand a high level of resilience—where raw, affective human interaction takes place—can only result in humiliation, frustration and outbursts of aggression.

A PIE OF QUOTIENTS

PHYSICAL INTELLECTUAL EMOTIONAL

Dealing with emotional fragility is about strengthening a person, and I shall be illustrating how this might be done in Part Two, Chapter 6. When a person feels strong in himself he will have no need to protect himself: he will become less aggressive.

SELF-ESTEEM

An aggressive child may appear to have a high opinion of himself, he may be arrogant and boastful. You could interpret this as a measure of his self-confidence.

You would be right in a certain respect. However, his excessively confident manner indicates that he is lacking self-esteem rather than being genuinely confident.

We all need self-esteem if we are to survive. The fragile child, for all the reasons we have mentioned so far, usually has a very poor opinion of himself. Indicators of low self-esteem are an inability to cope with failure, a dislike of new experiences, the need for constant reassurance and a poor opinion of one's physical appearance.

We have seen how we all use techniques to defend ourselves. The way in which we perceive ourselves determines our behaviour; we will do all we can to preserve a consistent self-image:

—If we do anything wrong we blame it on external factors beyond our control. When good things happen we try to take credit for them. We can never do any wrong.
—We always exaggerate the part we play in shaping events in which we have participated. We hype our own performance.
—We always assume that someone else is going to have to change, that the other person is always wrong.
—We invent personal handicaps before events occur in order to avoid failure. In other words, the excuses come before the event as a guarantee of safety.

Vulnerable personalities need to employ these mechanisms more than most; their behaviour therefore often appears to be inappropriate. They present as aggressive, bullying, obnoxious individuals.

How we feel about things affects our perception. Our

sense of identity relies on our perceiving events and crystallising them into a meaningful world. We do this by attaching feelings to events. Fragile personalities, because of their sensitivity, often ascribe a different set of feeling values to events; their perception of the world can thus be quite different from that of most people and we may find it difficult to understand their consequent behaviour.

All people behave in ways consistent with the perception they have of themselves. If you have an aggressive child you can be sure that he has a very poor opinion of himself. If he is aggressive, he will have labelled himself as such, and in order to maintain consistency the label will become self-fulfilling.

We cannot escape the physical shell in which we exist, and the image we have of it plays a large part in determining our behaviour. We know how we would like to appear and any deviation from this lowers our self-esteem. Attractive people gain favourable responses from others and this reinforces their attractiveness by enhancing their self-esteem: they become more confident. Less attractive children, and fat children in particular, are disliked by others, and if they are emotionally fragile to begin with they will behave inappropriately.

If children are insecure in relation to their body image they may retreat into sickness for protection. Their preoccupation with health problems enables them to avoid facing up to any comparison with others. They may present as being tired all the time rather than sick. This usually indicates unresolved emotional difficulties which centre around hostility towards a loved one, or guilt because in the face of their perceived physical state they have abandoned certain objectives. In either case the child has given up the race with regard to his ideal physical self-image.

We all choose to do what we think we can do. What a child believes he can do is critical to his performance. From his experiences he knows what he can do, and he builds on these and thus progresses. If he experiences failure early in his school life he will lack confidence and have little motivation to carry on. High self-esteem and the experience of success are mutually reinforcing. If a child has high self-esteem to begin with he will be less likely to be affected by

failure. The fragile child, however, is at great risk in the
early days of his schooling. He can quite easily fail and thereafter will continue to do so.

The second concept which helps to form my platform
of operations is therefore that of *self-esteem*—the first,
you remember, was *emotional fragility*. The two are intrinsically linked. If a child has a high level of self-esteem,
he will be resilient; if he has a low opinion of himself, he
will be vulnerable. Part of any strengthening process will
involve helping the child to crystallise his sense of identity.
You will need to help him to know the significant people,
places and events in his life, and what he thinks he stands
for. You will need to help him to create a more positive
picture of himself; to do this you should help him adopt a
more realistic ideal model. We shall deal with this in Part
Two, Chapter 6.

CONTROLS

There is a third factor threading through all my work with
aggressive children, which has both theoretical and practical
implications.

Most children who exhibit difficult behaviour have not
experienced an appropriate degree of external control. All
children need the security of having somebody else in
charge, and a child who is emotionally fragile needs more
protection than others. An aggressive child has less self-
control: he is impulsive. He needs someone to create a safe
environment for him, and before he can acquire self-control
he must have experienced these controls from outside himself.

There are many reasons why parents and others fail to
provide controls. The parents may simply be copying the
style of parenting which they experienced as a child. This
often happens. On the other hand, the parents themselves
may be fragile; they may not be able to make decisions.

Fragile personalities tend not to be pro-active: they
will not make their own way in life; they wait for circumstances to control their destiny. They feel helpless. Someone
else is responsible and someone else will make the moves.
As fragile people they do not imagine that they have any

responsibility for their behaviour. Their point of control is outside themselves.

Fragile parents tend to feel too much for their child. They live 'under his skin' and cannot see him as a separate individual whose needs are different from their own.

A lack of decision incurs an absence of rules and the child interprets this as a lack of strength. He flouts the weak parent and, in shame, becomes very angry. In the same way the deliberately permissive home promotes only a lack of respect and an increase in aggressive behaviour.

No child can be 'good' unless he has a clear set of rules which are consistently applied. His self-esteem cannot be enhanced unless there is some form of measurement for his performance; he cannot make amends when he gets it wrong if there is no avenue of restitution. Controls allow him to measure himself: he can put things right if he knows what he has done wrong. Matters can be resolved, rather than adding to his level of anxiety.

Aggressive children may, however, come from homes where the controls have been too heavy. If parents enforce rules without involving their children in any way they will promote a lack of conscience, or misery and withdrawal.

The home most conducive to the development of well-adjusted children is one in which the parents are in control, and their control is welcomed because it progressively involves the children in decision-making as they grow older. Young children who are fragile will need the protection of external controls for a longer period of time. If the controls have been effectively applied their inherent value system will be used by the child for the rest of his life. They will provide him with consistent anchor points for his attitudes and performance.

Disabled children such as those who are emotionally vulnerable will always tend to rely on external controls. If you provide these you will be allowing them to enjoy a period when they might gain positive reinforcement for their behaviour. When they have experienced success they will be stimulated to achieving; then you will have begun the process whereby they can start to feel in control of their own lives.

Professionals sometimes believe that the aggressive

child needs a friend, that he feels unwanted and unloved. They set out to offer love and friendship, and somehow this does not involve making decisions for him. They are making a grave mistake. The child sees them as another adult who has no strength. He cannot rely on them. Accordingly he manipulates them to cater for the immediate gratification of his needs. He will smile and behave well when things are going his way, but when he is refused something the care worker or teacher will soon realise the limitations of the friendship. Meaningful relationships can only develop with aggressive children when the adult has assumed the expected role. The child expects him to be in control, to assume responsibility for him, not to be on the same level as one of his friends. When the child knows that the adult is there for him in this way he will respond. He will become more compliant and his aggression will diminish.

Achieving this kind of controlling and caring relationship is difficult unless you are clear about the level and kind of controlling mechanisms with which you may feel at ease.

Physical Control
Many children have been abused both emotionally and physically. One form of abuse rarely recognised, however, is to deny their need for control. Aggressive children often need to be physically restrained in the interests of their own safety or the safety of others, or merely held for the security this may give them. It would be irresponsible not to recognise this.

Professionals and parents are wary of physically controlling aggressive children for fear of accusations of abuse which may be made against them. This is a regrettable state of affairs. If medical practitioners were denied the use of penicillin there would be an outcry. To deny children the comfort of knowing that somebody is in charge of their raging emotions should in itself be classed as abuse.

The situation has been distorted by the reaction of the public and the media to the behaviour of a minority of deviant child care workers and educationalists. Any form of treatment or techniques can and will be abused by such people. The possibility of this occurring has now been greatly minimised by Child Protection Procedures; an intrinsic part of these is the belief that a child has rights, and his right to be physically protected is built into them.

If you are confused about what form of physical control is acceptable, then there is a good guiding principle: question your intent. If you intend to harm the child or to punish him physically, you will be prosecuted under the Child Protection Procedures. If you intend to help him, to protect him from damaging himself, others or property, then your physical intervention and restraining techniques will be acceptable.

Medication

In cases of persistent violent aggression a child may be controlled by medication. Any decision to administer medication must be made in the knowledge that there is little evidence of drug treatment programmes being curative: conditions can merely be controlled. In the short term this may be acceptable, but in the long term there are serious doubts about the impact of numerous side effects. For example, severe cases of aggression may be treated with lithium, but the side effects include nausea, vomiting, thirst and urinary frequency.

Part of any drug programme should be the withdrawal of the treatment at suitable intervals, in order that the continuing need for its administration can be assessed, and this procedure in itself may cause difficulties.

Pioneering work is being undertaken in relation to the possibility of a genetic and physiological basis for excessive aggression in children, but at the time of writing the general rule should be to treat all such approaches as experimental. Treating an aggressive child with drugs should be considered only in extreme circumstances, where the child is in a continual state of misery and risk because of his condition.

Decision-making

Emotionally disturbed children have a distorted perception of the world and need someone to look after them. This involves caring for them physically and making decisions about their education and welfare.

Because of the current emphasis on children's rights there is a tendency to over-involve the child in decision-making. Important decisions are often left to him: the emotionally fragile child is supposed to be able to say what he thinks will be best for him. If he shows resistance to a course of action, it may be regarded as a violation of his rights if he is overruled. It is as though our society has abdicated all responsibility for our children. Children do need to take part in decision-making and in rule-making, but we should never forget that we aggravate their condition when we let them feel there is nobody else in charge.

The involvement of children in discussion of their particular problem highlights the level of abuse that is inflicted on them in the name of 'children's rights'. In the child's presence professionals and parents may talk at great length about his problems, and as he listens he may absorb their opinions. If they say negative things about him he will have negative aspects of his self-image reinforced; if they say positive things about him he is likely to exaggerate their value.

Even if he does not understand their opinions his self-esteem will be distorted. To sit and listen to people talk about your behaviour and personality can be a devastating experience for the mature adult; for the vulnerable child it can only be regarded as mindless abuse. It may encourage him to be even more egocentric; in the young child it could lead to an undue amount of introspection and self-analysis. Children should really be leading their lives and not talking about them.

Parents and professionals should realise that they are adults. They should not presume that they are on the same level as a child, or that he is able to think as they do. His whole world is different. He thinks as a child, they think as an adult or as a parent. Should they begin to think as a child or he attempt to think as a parent, we have a recipe for disaster. Adults should understand how a child may be thinking, to appreciate his logic and feelings; in the light of these and their own experience and wisdom, they should make mature decisions, however uncomfortable these may be.

Adults and parents have a role to fulfil—to make decisions. They should recognise the need of the emotionally fragile child for someone to take decisions for him. They should also recognise the damage that can be done to a child by an excessive amount of mature conceptual analysis in his presence.

LABELS

In an attempt to feel that they are somehow released from any implied responsibility, and in their desire to feel that the condition of the aggressive child is controllable, parents and professionals will often try to give his behaviour a label. This endows the child with the respectability of a medical condition rather than the stigma of a psychological state. We should be aware of this, because once a label has been attached to a child it implies a fixed set of characteristics which will often become self-fulfilling: the parent or professional will have a level of expectation based on them, and should the child understand the label he may assume the expected patterns of behaviour, adopting the attitude that he has the condition and nothing can be done about it.

Attention Deficit Hyperactivity Disorder (ADHD)

Many aggressive children may be labelled as suffering from Attention Deficit Hyperactivity Disorder. Children who are so described are easily distractible. They are restless and have a short attention span. They are impulsive and can be destructive and aggressive.

Many experts regard such behaviour as a sign of neurological dysfunction and support the use of an amphetamine (Ritalin) to control the condition, thus enabling a child to receive an education until he maturates through this developmental condition.

The consensus of opinion, however, is that a child who requires Ritalin also requires Special Education where he can receive intensive training in social skills; his parents should also be given support and advice on how to manage the condition at home.

An alternative, non-medical, approach, should be to consider the child with ADHD as emotionally fragile, especially perhaps with regard to his hyperactivity.

We said earlier that many emotionally fragile children cannot operate on an affective level. Because of their sensitivity they cannot cope with the closeness of a family. In the family setting the child who is sensitive and tends towards hyperactivity can be overstimulated. Parents of hyperactive children usually presume that the children are highly intelligent and need their minds expanding. They think that if they can push the child, his energies will dissipate. However, all the time that the adults have been trying to push the child he has been ahead of them. He has in effect been in charge—and they will never catch up. He will keep going until the cows come home, or until somebody strikes out in frustration.

In extreme cases of hyperactivity the child should be removed from the close family setting and placed in a semi-neutral emotional environment, providing a regime of routines and firm controls, where he will be able to operate without the complications of any affective demands. In his new setting he should be clear about who is in charge and they should be aware of his needs. He may well appear to be highly intelligent and in need of stimulation, but before he can use his intelligence he needs to calm down and stabilise. He will do this if he is aware that someone has taken control of his life.

This should be seen as the priority, and great attention given to providing a regular daily schedule for him. He needs to be dampened down, not kept stimulated. He does not need to expand, he needs to retract.

This may seem to be an obvious thing to say when trying to combat hyperactivity, but it needs to be said. Too often people attempt to exhaust hyperactive children by constantly stimulating them. They are fighting a losing battle; and if they believe that the natural intelligence of their child needs to be developed then they are going the wrong way about it.

If a hyperactive child remains in the home, then the parents should recognise the importance of clarifying their objectives. If they want him to become less distracted and impulsive they will need to work out a routine for him, to which they should adhere quite rigidly. In cases of decision-taking *they* should be the ones who usually decide; they should never feel that the child is leading them. It is a good idea, for example, when they find it difficult to make a decision, for them to say 'no'. If they cannot logically justify their decision it may acquire an even greater potency: their position of power and control will be asserted. It is impor-tant, of course, that this kind of unilateral action does not take place too regularly, otherwise the child's frustration will result in an increase in restlessness, impulsiveness and aggression.

This kind of firm controlling will always be counter-productive unless it is accompanied by praise and encouragement when the child is behaving appropriately. It should also be accompanied by shared activities. Parents and professionals will only receive positive responses from the child when he feels that they like him and enjoy doing things with him. His unacceptable behaviour must be regarded as such; he should not feel rejected because of it. A central aim should be to make him feel good about himself, not the opposite.

Accepting the concept of emotional fragility and recognising the consequent need of the aggressive child for clear external controls and an enhanced feeling of self-worth, it is possible to devise an effective programme for the hyper-active child.

Learning Difficulties

Children who have difficulty in learning may have some degree of brain damage; they may have limited intellectual ability. A common form of learning disorder occurs in reading, whereby children who experience difficulty are described as dyslexic. This term covers a cluster of symptoms and the evidence seems to point to the fact that there is a physiological and genetic basis for the condition.

However, it should not be presumed that, because there is evidence of a biological condition, other factors do not play a part in the learning disorder. Children with a biological impairment may be more vulnerable to adverse environmental factors than other children. They may, to begin with, be less resilient.

There are many children with a variety of learning difficulties who are not intellectually impaired or physically disabled. We should recognise that these children are emotionally fragile. For whatever reason, they are anxious to the point where they cannot retain information and build on previous knowledge.

If we remember the concept of fragility and the need of every child for a sense of self-worth and external control, we should be able to dissipate a large part of this anxiety. We should see that if a child cannot read he may be more anxious than others; perhaps he needs more time on an extended readiness programme; perhaps we should forget reading skills and concentrate more on what he *can* do, and wait for his confidence to build up. When he is stronger in himself he will be able to learn. He is continually worried about failure; when he looks at the mistake in his exercise book his self is revealed: he rips out the page at the slightest blemish.

It is easy to imagine that learning difficulties can be alleviated by slower, repeated instructions or by some unusual techniques. If the problem is to be truly addressed we should recognise the underlying cause. Children who cannot read or understand mathematical problems are anxious about failure because of their fragility and low self-esteem. One must be careful not to give them an even greater sense of failure.

Parents and professionals should keep these central concerns at the forefront of their minds. All children would learn more effectively if they felt that they themselves came before subject-matter and examination results. Vulnerable children in particular can be damaged beyond repair—a fact borne out by the increased level of disturbed behaviour which begins when children start school.

CONCLUSION

A fresh approach can be taken with your aggressive child if you have begun to think about all the issues raised in this part of the book. You will already have moved out of the enmeshed situation which so many people are drawn into by the aggressive child. If, as a professional, you have not yet started working with such children, you will hopefully avoid becoming emotionally involved. There is a great tendency to presume that difficult children need someone to be close to: it would be a mistake to see that as your role.

I hope you have begun to apply the concept of emotional fragility to your situation whatever it may be, and that you can see clearly that the way you reacted to your life situation has been largely determined by your emotional quotient. Should you accept the concept, you should also recognise that a person can learn to live with it, as with any other disability, and that as any other quotient it can be enhanced.

Part Two

HELPING THE AGGRESSIVE CHILD

1 Question Time

Having thought about all the issues discussed in Part One, you should now have a good understanding of the behaviour of your aggressive child: your understanding will be the basis for a plan of action.

We have seen how much aggressive behaviour is caused by children misinterpreting the behaviour of others. They see the world from the viewpoint of a fragile personality and their relationship to it is based on highly defensive reactions. We all have our perception of the world and, depending on our emotional state, we interpret it as being either friendly or hostile. Those who are coping well with life have everything nicely balanced; but we all relate to the world according to the peaks and troughs of our emotions. Some of us are more fragile to begin with: the more fragile we are, the more sensitive we will be to our circumstances. The peaks and troughs experienced by fragile personalities are more severe than those experienced by those who are resilient.

It is important to realise that aggressive children are not the only ones to have their own perception of the world. When you are dealing with difficult children you should always take into account your own emotional state. It may be that the behaviour of the aggressive child has been largely determined by your level of anxiety.

When dealing with these children your apprehension may be so great that they fulfil your expectations. Remember that they are extremely sensitive and may react violently to any feeling of insecurity. If you perceive them as a threat, there is a good chance that you will provoke an aggressive outburst; if you see and interpret their behaviour differently, you may find that their behaviour shifts according to your attitude.

A great deal of our apprehension of aggressive children is caused by ignorance. We are not sure how we feel about them, or how we feel about ourselves when faced with one of their outbursts. We are not sure what it is that makes us feel as we do when we have been through one of these traumatic experiences.

The first piece of practical work will therefore consist of answering a number of questions, since the secret of most human problems can be found in the dictum 'know thyself'. I hope that you will answer the questions seriously, and afterwards read my comments. The questions may seem trite and of no value; they are intended to help you think deeply about yourself, so take your time in answering them. The more deeply you think, the more you will feel able to crystallise your personal approach to your aggressive child.

There is therefore no time limit to the questions and exercises. I would suggest, however, that if you answer a question in less than five minutes you are missing a golden opportunity to get to know yourself just that little bit better.

It is important for you to read all the questions and my comments, even though some questions are addressed to specific people. If you do this you may come to a greater appreciation of the way others see the aggressive child. Use a notepad or sheets of paper for your answers.

One more point: you are not allowed to use yes and no answers.

QUESTION ONE: TO PARENTS AND OTHERS

Do you see your aggressive child as:
1   domineering and loud?
2   a disappointment?
3   an embarrassment?
4   a nuisance?
5   frightening?

Comments
1   If you see your child as domineering and loud I presume he makes you feel weak.

If you feel weak in his presence it may be because you need to see him differently. He somehow embroils you in his unsettled state, and you become lost in it.

We shall discuss how to approach this later in the chapter.

2   If you see your child as a disappointment it may be that from the very beginning you had false expectations of him.

All parents have a mental picture of how they would like their child to grow up. There is also a tendency for them to relive their lives through their children. Some parents do this more than others.

If you have a fixed idea of what you would like your child to be, then you will either be disappointed or, if he conforms, he may be unfulfilled.

Children should be regarded as individuals, emotionally attached but increasingly separate from their parents. Parents should recognise also that their children will continually change.

Your child may behave aggressively if you have expectations of him which are beyond his capabilities.

His present behaviour may be a disappointment to you, but if you are to understand him you should ask whether his behaviour is merely a reaction to your unrealistic demands, or a reflection of your own sense of failure in life. If you are unhappy with your lot, there is a good chance that you will inflict your disappointment on him.

3   If you see your child as an embarrassment it is clear that you see him as part of yourself.

You should not do this. If you persist in seeing your difficult child as an extension of yourself you will become more and more frustrated. He is a separate, unique individual who is related to you through birth. You care for and love him, but you are not responsible for his characteristic vulnerability.

If you see your child as an embarrassment you are not seeing him as a disabled child; you are somehow seeing him as a creation of the devil, someone with whom you do not wish to be associated. You should see your child's behaviour as a symptom of his fragility. He has to learn how to cope with this and you have to help him.

You should see his disablement as needing to be explained to your friends. You will have to do this if you are to succeed in helping him. If you take time to explain his difficulties to others there should be no need for you to feel embarrassed. When you are explaining matters to them, be careful not to do it in front of the child. We discussed the harmful effects of this in Part One, Chapter 6.

4   If you see your aggressive child getting in the way of other things which you may wish to do you are seeing him as a nuisance and this is clearly not the way to make him feel good.

However, if you wish to see his behaviour improve, you yourself must have some strong personal interests other than him. There are some very good reasons for this: if he dominates your life you will sink with him; if you stand for something else then your sense of identity will be a strength not only to yourself but to him.

If you have no personal interests, see this as needing immediate attention. Do not be afraid of your child's reaction when you first attend that nightclass, or when you first go jogging. Unless you become stronger in yourself you will never be able to help him. If you have recruited friends to help you (see Part Two, Chapter 2), you will have explained this plan of action to them and they will have realised that it is part of a definite strategy.

It is important for your child to realise that he is not at the centre of the universe. Fragile personalities tend to think this, and others accommodate them. If you really care for your child you will see it as your duty to do something separate from him. You need to see yourself as being something more than an exhausted and frustrated parent; he needs to see you as someone who has strength; he will sense this if he knows of your other interests in life.

He will of course feel rejected when you first leave him, but if you are going with the interests of both of you in mind, then with time the strategy will work. If you see him as a nuisance you will neither leave nor return to him in the right frame of mind: you will be faced with an escalation of aggressive behaviour and you will soon lose your helpers.

You may say that you will lose your helpers because your child will relish the thought of you going out and that he will lead them a merry dance on your departure.

This kind of thinking will get you nowhere. You are back at square one, with your life centring around your highly manipulative and demanding child. You must put yourself first before he can begin to receive your help.

Prepare your helpers and take the risk. Ask yourself what will happen to your child if you do not.

5 If you see your child as frightening, then it is clear that you have lost control, over him and over yourself. You must begin by gaining control over yourself.

Start with these exercises. You will find it very useful to go through them with a close friend. A good way to do them is for you each to complete them on your own and then to discuss them with each other. Sharing can make you stronger.

EXERCISE ONE
Answer the following questions:
  1 Can you remember where you lived at the time of your child's birth, and how you felt when you first held him?
  2 Can you remember the first time you took him for a walk in his pushchair or pram?
  3 Can you remember where he took his first step?
  4 When did your troubles seem to begin?
  5 Did something happen which might have changed the way you saw your child?

EXERCISE TWO
Write down the dates and details of the three most critical points in your life, the three most important crossroads.
  1 Crisis number one:
  2 Crisis number two:
  3 Crisis number three:
Take your time in remembering these. Remember where you were and who you were with. Try to go back into these times. Remember how you felt.

Where did your child fit into these events? Was he born before them or afterwards? Was he part of the scenario?

It is important for you to look at your life closely. You may not think that this is relevant to the matter in hand, but if you are feeling that your child is out of control you must accept that it could be you who are weak. You have lost the strength to exert control over your child because you have perhaps lost faith in yourself.

I would like you to do a further exercise. It is simple but could take up to thirty minutes to complete. Do not rush. The more detail you can include, the more effective the exercise will be.

EXERCISE THREE
Complete the following for yourself, *not* for your child:

Name:

Date of birth: Place of birth:
Weight at birth: Baptised at:
Mother's name: Father's name:
Brothers' names: Sisters' names:

1   Schools attended, with dates:
2   Names of favourite teachers:
3   The worst thing that happened to me at school:
4   How my mother would have described me:
5   My greatest achievement:
6   My first job:
7   My first boss:
8   My favourite pastime:
9   Three places I have enjoyed visiting:
10 The worst thing that I have ever done:
11 The funniest thing that ever happened to me:
12 Where I was, who I was living with and what I was doing at the age of
  a   ten years:
  b   twenty years:
  c   twenty-one years:
  d   twenty-two years:
  e   twenty-three years:
  f   twenty-four years:
  g   twenty-five years:
  h   thirty years:
  i   thirty-five years:
  j   forty years:
  k   forty-five years:
  l   fifty years:
  m   at the present:

13   The most important people in my whole life (at least
      three):
14   They are important to me because:

Having completed these exercises you should be aware that
your past life can offer you a great deal of strength. Although
you may feel that your life has been mundane, it has been
unique and is far more complex than you would at first
imagine. You have lived through a great deal. I hope that
as you tried to complete the questions you discovered this.

   More importantly, I hope that in attempting the exercise
you realised that you have a wealth of experience to draw
upon—a source of strength.

   The exercises may also have helped you to understand your
aggressive child. You may have appreciated that the state of
your affairs could have been too much for him to cope with;
you may have discovered in looking at your past that you were
not so different from him when you were a child.

   None of this should upset you: if you can look at your
past and not be afraid of it, you will feel stronger and better
able to cope with your aggressive child. You will understand
him, but more importantly, you will begin to understand
yourself. I hope that if you did not share this experience
with someone you will have the courage to do so later. You
will find that it will help you enormously.

QUESTION TWO: TO TEACHERS AND OTHERS

Is the focus of your teaching:
   1   teaching your subject specialism?
   2   children's learning difficulties?
   3   children's behaviour patterns?

Comments
1   If you focus on teaching your specialism and see your
role as ensuring that all your children complete the curriculum, you will be creating severe discipline problems for
yourself.

   Children are human beings and need to be recognised as
such, not treated as material passing through a system. If they
are to be motivated to work, they need you to greet them as

they enter the classroom, to give words of praise and encouragement to all—not forgetting those whom you would expect to be able to manage work on their own—and to show an interest in their personal affairs outside the classroom.

All children have a capacity to learn and you should see yourself as being there to make learning possible. You should not see your role as an expert who is there only to impart knowledge.

It is usually a good idea to see the imparting of knowledge as a bonus. If you take this approach you will find that it becomes considerably easier to motivate your pupils. The curriculum will be covered more effectively in that pupils will return your respect and work for you, rather than becoming bored with your subject-matter. When they are bored they will behave badly and aggressively to each other and to you.

The preparation of stimulating material will be to no avail unless you focus on each child's need for recognition.

EXERCISE ONE
I would like you to write down the names of the first six pupils in your class and for each of them list the following information (do not refer to anyone else):

Full name (include middle name):
Birthday:
Address:
Father's occupation:
Names of brothers and sisters:
Other schools attended:
Closest school friend:
Favourite TV programme:
Favourite food:
Favourite football team:
Favourite pop star:
Main hobby:
Last holiday venue:
His ambition:

If you can provide this information for the first six on the register, without having to refer to anyone, then you are approaching your teaching in the correct way.

If you cannot provide the information, you will most likely be experiencing some difficulties. At the very least, you are not seeing your pupils working to their full potential.

You should find out personal background information by taking time to talk to your pupils. They need you to take an interest in their lives, not simply to be there as some kind of mystical guru. The enthusiasm for your specialism is an important part of your appeal, but before the children can begin to learn they need to see you as a person. To achieve this, it is up to you to take an interest in them.

2   If, when you are teaching, you are focusing on the difficulties that children may be experiencing, then you will be seeing yourself in the correct role.

Given a good curriculum, stimulating material, an enthusiastic specialist, and someone who takes a genuine interest in their affairs, most pupils will still have difficulties in understanding certain concepts and processes.

You should see your role as being there to recognise when this happens; not to be there to complain when it does. Many teachers fall into the trap of thinking of pupils who are having difficulties as nuisances. Things would somehow be different if only this or that child were not there. The assumption is that it is possible to have a group of children who all perform at a standardised level. They might all be equally capable on a theoretical basis, but in terms of actual performance this never happens because of the many factors we have discussed in Part One.

You will find that if you are focusing on children's learning difficulties, they will interpret your interest as concern for them as people. You will be minimising the possibility of any behavioural problems.

EXERCISE TWO
Take the bottom three names from a class list and complete the following for each:

Name:
   1   Learning style:
   2   Areas of weakness:
   3   Areas of strength:

The more detailed the assessment you were able to give, the more evident is your interest in learning difficulties. If you are keeping accurate records you will have a good idea of the capabilities of each child and be able to expand on the details required in the above exercise. It is when you are ignorant of a child's capabilities that your level of expectation is unreasonable. A sensitive child cannot cope with failure, and he will react defensively if he feels threatened in this way. It is vitally important, therefore, to be aware of his attainment levels, and to set work which can give him a chance to succeed.

If you are truly concentrating on the learning difficulties of a child, you will be keeping an accurate and up-to-date record of his performance, highlighting areas where difficulty is being experienced.

3   If you focus on the behaviour patterns of your children you will often find that they are linked to learning processes. If a child is becoming frustrated because he cannot understand something, he will be restless and will start to misbehave. He will fool around with his classmates and do all he can to disrupt the proceedings.

Emotionally fragile children will often be unable to retain information because of their level of anxiety. Although they may be intelligent they will be unable to build on retained knowledge. They may also have learning blocks created by the association of negative experiences in certain subject areas.

If you see your role as a keen observer of behaviour you will be able to prevent explosive outbursts. The longer a child can go without an aggressive outburst the better chance he has of experiencing the pleasure of behaving in a socially acceptable manner.

Seeing children's behaviour as an indicator of their learning processes is therefore a very important part of teaching. It is equally important to see their behaviour as a possible reflection of your own.

In Question One the point was made to parents that it is vital for adults to be honest about the contribution they might be making to a child's behaviour. If you are loud and bullying, or if your style is autocratic, then you will breed

BEFORE YOU CAN

FOCUS

ON

YOUR CHILD

YOU MUST

FOCUS

ON

YOURSELF

the same kind of attitude in your pupils. Children who tend to be aggressive will imitate your style; others may be scarred for life by your overpowering manner.

If you are firm and fair in your controls, and if you combine this with a genuine interest not only in the work of the children, but also in their lives, then you will truly motivate them. They will present you with few behavioural difficulties.

EXERCISE THREE

A Take a class list and for each of the pupils complete the following:
  1 Name:
  2 Behaviour (one-word description):
  3 Degree of consistency in this behaviour:
      Always:
      Periodically:
      Specifically when:
      Specifically when not:
B Name the child who causes you most concern:
  1 State his principal behavioural characteristic:
  2 Describe the worst thing that he has ever done:
  3 Describe the worst thing that he could possibly do:

You may be surprised at the descriptions you gave and at how difficult it was to describe the behaviour of some children. You should give more attention to those children whom you have described rather blandly. It is these middle-of-the-road children who tend to be forgotten, and they will become bored and demotivated unless you pay special importance to them.

On completing this exercise you may have realised that the behaviour of most children is consistent. In a way this is a good sign—especially if they are consistently well behaved and appear to be happy. However, if their behaviour is consistently of concern to you, you should examine whether you have given enough attention to the matters described in this chapter. If you feel that you have given the child due attention and that you have made special allowances for any problems indicated in his test data, then you may need to refer to a specialist. The child could, for example, be permanently depressed or pervasively agitated and in need of professional help.

If you feel that a child has severe mood swings you should check to see whether they relate to other events. It would then be a simple matter of seeing how you could rearrange things to avoid his negative reactions.

If you conclude that the mood changes are severe and unpredictable, you might begin by considering the central proposition of this book, that some children are emotionally fragile: they will react to subtle changes which may not be apparent to you.

It is useful to write down precisely what it is that concerns you when you think of a particular aggressive child. You may find that you cannot place your finger on it. In these instances it is worth having another look at yourself. You should question whether or not you have prejudices which may be getting in the way when it comes to relating to him. When you do discover what it is that causes you concern it may help you to do something about it. Having read Part One, you may now see that you can actually understand the worst thing that your aggressive child has ever done; you may also feel that the worst thing he could ever do is less of a threat to you. Asking what the worst scenario might be can often put to rest your fantasies and fears.

QUESTION THREE: TO PARENTS AND PROFESSIONALS

When an episode of aggression occurs do you feel:
1   emotionally involved?
2   out of control?
3   ashamed and incompetent?

Comments
1   Parents in particular become emotionally involved when their aggressive child has an outburst. It would be worrying if they did not, since it would imply that there was little bonding between them. Professionals likewise find it difficult to control their automatic response to aggression.

However, it is important for you all to appreciate that when dealing with an aggressive child you will only promote his pattern of behaviour by reacting in an emotional manner.

Fragile children are unable to relate appropriately to people on a feeling level. From an early age they have reacted with aggression when expected to 'connect', and they have become used to a pattern of intense hostile relationships with others. When you meet them you will be faced with this way of relating, and if you comply you will only be escalating the child's condition.

You should not feel guilty about reacting to the child on an emotional level: you can do nothing about your physiological make-up. Be aware, however, of the need to resist becoming involved in his dynamics. A good idea is to imagine yourself wearing a white coat: you are a professional in charge of a case. You need to look at all the facts objectively.

It is difficult for parents to remain detached and it is for this reason that the family setting is not always the most appropriate for the aggressive child.

2 If you feel out of control when dealing with an aggressive child you should first look at yourself. Parents have already done this in Question One and I would refer professionals to that section.

It is of critical importance that the aggressive child be given external controls. If you are not strong enough to provide these, do not see it as a reflection of incompetence and feel guilty about it. The theme of this chapter is about taking an honest look at yourself. You must be frank about your weaknesses as well as your strengths. Schools and children's homes can only operate safely and efficiently if staff are open with each other about their capabilities. If staff do not declare their weaknesses then they cannot be given support; children will suffer the consequences.

If you are not clear about the kind of controls you should be using you should consult the head of your school or home. Children are protected by law from controls which may be construed as being abusive or against their rights. I give guidelines on this matter in Part Two, Chapter 3.

3 If you feel ashamed when a child has an aggressive outburst, you have either a distorted perception of your role or the wrong perception of the child's condition.

I have already discussed this issue with parents (Question One). Teachers and child care workers often think that everyone expects them to have perfect control over their charges from morning until night. They feel ashamed and humiliated when a child has an aggressive outburst, even when his condition is acknowledged.

You should not feel ashamed when a child has an outburst unless you know that you have been negligent.

Because of the variable nature of the human condition it is not possible to predict all behaviour and so outbursts are going to occur despite the very best preparation. You should therefore appreciate that crises are expected to occur; you should not be in the business of hiding them. To be ashamed implies that you do not recognise that a child who behaves aggressively is disabled; you still think of him as an evil person, a thorough nuisance.

If your perception of him is that he has a fragile personality and that his disablement is indicated by a persistent need to defend himself, then you will not be ashamed or humiliated when his condition becomes apparent.

It is a feature of our society that it accords stigma to disablement; it is even more deplorable that it completely rejects disablement when it has no apparent physical basis. As a professional you should not share the same prejudices.

CONCLUSION

Exercises are about strengthening; I hope that you found time to do the short exercises in this chapter.

If you are going to be able to work effectively with difficult, aggressive children you will need to feel strong in yourself.

By reading Part One you will already have begun to look at the aggressive child more objectively. You will, I hope, see him as a weak, disabled child who often appears in a gorilla costume. Being able to see behind the antics should have strengthened you.

If you have done the exercises in this chapter you will have examined your perception of the aggressive child and how he makes you feel; you will have begun to put your feelings and perceptions into perspective. As a professional you should have come to some conclusions about the focus of your work and how you might adjust this to avoid confrontations and aggressive outbursts.

Although some of the questions were separately addressed to parents and professionals, the hope was that you would read them all and consider the comments. Parents and professionals should try to understand each other's positions.

Professionals are too keen to lay the blame for a child's behaviour at the parents' door; parents will often complain that their child only began behaving aggressively when he started school. Both parties should get out of the habit of blaming; blaming only happens when you are in a state of panic, when you feel helpless.

Schools should take the initiative and arrange regular support meetings for parents of children who are presenting difficult behaviour. These parents are usually only invited to school in order that the Head can complain about their child. This is very wrong. In schools where parents have been given positive support there has been a dramatic decrease in the number of aggressive episodes.

Professionals should understand how exhausted parents can become when they have a difficult child. They have often become isolated because of their child's behaviour. The school could provide them with the support they need. If the parents can be strengthened then they will be able to control their children, the children will feel more secure and their behaviour will change.

Some parents need help with actual child-rearing techniques; most just need to feel that there is somebody on their side.

On the other hand, parents should appreciate the demands made on teachers and child care workers and not presume that as professionals they automatically know all the answers. For every problem that a child presents there are at least six possible courses of action to be taken and the effectiveness of none can be guaranteed. The work of professionals is complicated because of the unique chemistry which each child presents.

2 Preparing for Action

You have attempted to prepare for action by looking inwards a little, and now you must look around you to ensure that you have done all you can to diminish the possibility of episodes of aggression occurring. If you have prepared yourself as thoroughly as possible it would be a shame if you were not to take advantage of a few strategic moves which might improve your chance of success.

Before discussing the way in which the child's setting may be adjusted to make your task easier, there are two other small points to make in relation to yourself.

A prerequisite for effective action is your liking for the child. He will sense whether you like him or not. If you do not like him then it would be worth arranging for someone else to work with him. Professionals may of course find this easier than parents, but it is more probable that a professional rather than a parent may dislike a child.

You should not be afraid to say that you find a child unlikeable: personalities do clash. It may be that at your stage of development you are unable to cope with the demands that a certain child might make on you. Be honest in your appraisal of the situation, because unless you like the child and are strong enough to cope with him he will feel that you are rejecting him rather than his behaviour when it comes to controlling mechanisms. If it is clear to him that you do like him, then you will find that he interprets your interventions as an indication of your care for him.

You need to have all the qualities of a good doctor: the child should be able to trust you both for your warmth and for your objectivity. He should feel safe with you because of the consistency of your approach.

A second prerequisite is for you to be capable of interpreting the child's behaviour and knowing when you need to do something about it. The skill employed is similar to the essential skill in driving a car: you need to be able to anticipate. If you can assess his behaviour accurately you will know when it is essential for you to intervene. It is not easy to learn this skill. Much of an aggressive child's behaviour is not harmful. He may fling his arms about or shout, but if he is not harming himself or others you should question whether it would be better to save your controls for when they might be used to greater effect. When he does act in a loud and objectionable manner, ask yourself if it is only you who objects. If it is only you, do not be afraid to tell him; if you are allowing him to be loud because you do not mind and nobody else is involved, tell him so. But never suffer in silence. The child needs to know that someone else is in charge and that if he is being loud and awkward then it is only because he is being allowed to be so.

I have divided this chapter up into sections relating primarily to teachers and to parents. However, both they and child care workers would benefit from reading all the sections, since the chapter is about understanding and sharing the way in which we can make adjustments in the interests of the aggressive child. Child care workers in particular need to read the whole chapter since they are often expected to take on the dual role of both parent and teacher.

ADJUST THE SETTING

Your purpose in adjusting either your home or your classroom should be to create an environment where there is little opportunity for the aggressive child to be at the mercy of his impulses. This may involve considering the nature of household or classroom equipment and furniture. It may also involve examining the chemistry of the group of children or adults with whom he is expected to interact; it may mean taking a very careful look at the activities which make up his day at school or at home.

a The Classroom

1 *Furnishings and Equipment*
Each item of equipment or furniture should be considered in the light of its potential misuse by the aggressive child. Although it is not possible to lock up everything that could

be used as a weapon, you should be thinking along these lines. You should be aware that certain items in particular could inflict serious harm on someone if he suddenly had one of his outbursts. If you are consciously thinking of these possibilities, then your skills of anticipation will be considerably enhanced.

It is a good idea to announce where children are allowed to go and what items of equipment they are allowed to use. Do not complain about a child's behaviour if you have not explained the rules: you are assuming that he can make them, and he cannot. Do not complain if you have to explain the rules many times to the aggressive child: we shall come to this problem later in the chapter when a solution will be proposed. Suffice to say at this stage that actions speak louder than words and that with highly manipulative, fragile and defensive children you may talk for ever to no effect. You must face them with consequences.

Another good idea is for children to have their own private storage facilities and their own space. The aggressive child will himself benefit enormously from this. He needs his possessions and his territory more than most. Often his possessions will mean more to him than people. It is worth appreciating this when you are trying to remove an object from him; it will certainly make you ask yourself whether you really need to do so.

As the aggressive child finds it difficult to cope with others, it is a good idea always to have at least three booths for personal study in the classroom. For economy these can be made from cardboard refrigerator packaging, with desks placed inside them. Many of us find it difficult to study with people around us; fragile children are easily distracted and benefit enormously from such a private facility. Three booths rather than one are suggested: it is important that a variety of children use them—but none as punishment. With imagination the booths can become an attraction for all pupils; the aggressive child will use them according to his need for a private space.

Do not persist in your expectation that he should be able to get on with the others; the fact is that he cannot and you should recognise this as a handicap. Would you expect a child with one leg to take part in a cross-country run? When the aggressive child is strong enough in himself he will feel able to integrate; you cannot force him to do so. Make sure, therefore, that you provide facilities for him to work on his own.

Aggressive children are highly impulsive: you would be doing them a great disservice if you were to pay no attention to adjusting the surroundings to meet their needs. If you left a sharp knife around and the child grabbed it in one of his outbursts, he could well seal his fate for life. If he did not go so far as this, the least that could happen would be that his self-image would suffer a serious setback. You are there to prevent this happening, to provide a setting in which he can experience progressively more extensive periods of calmness and stability. You are there to enhance his self-esteem, not give him opportunities to erode it.

Although the furnishings and equipment should be designed and arranged for the physical safety of the aggressive child, you must bear in mind the tremendous impact that good-quality furnishings can have on the behaviour of children. If their physical environment is pleasant there is a good chance that it will be reflected in the children's behaviour. Carpets and soft lighting can have a dramatic effect on the behaviour of fragile children in particular; perhaps it is the warmth and sense of caring that comes with them.

2   *The Group Setting*
As a classroom teacher you may not be the one to decide which children are in your group, but you can try to arrange them so that the chemistry stands a chance of success. Careful study of the personalities in your group may make it possible for you to see where the aggressive child could be placed to minimise the chance of an outburst. Often a child may react particularly badly with another one, and simply by rearranging the seating the problem is solved.

By altering the sub-groups in the class you may find that the aggressive child becomes less so. It is in the interests of all the children for their groups to be changed from time to time, but for the aggressive child it can be an extremely useful opportunity for a fresh start. If you do rearrange the groups, do not single him out; if the whole class is not to be changed around, then move at least three other children. If the aggressive child is working well in his group it is better that any changes should be minimal. He will prefer it if no changes are ever made; it will be up to you to look at the chemistry of the group setting and make objective decisions as to how it can best operate. Always be on the lookout for ways in which you can alter the setting in order to improve his chance of remaining calm; never presume that you have to put up with the status quo. You could ask yourself whether it is you rather than the child who cannot take the risk that is incurred with change.

3 *Activities*

The aggressive child will be easily distracted; he will have a short span of concentration and because of his anxiety he will find it difficult to retain information. When you plan his work you must bear all this in mind. If he is restless and behaving badly it will be because he has been distracted by something else, because he cannot do the work or because the task set for him was too long.

You must ensure that he is in a position where the amount of distraction is minimal, that the work you have given him is pitched at the correct level and that you have broken the work up into short stages. The aggressive child needs to be able to achieve quick success; he is incapable of staying on task for very long.

Your classroom may need to be upgraded to cater for his needs. Secondary school classrooms in particular are often simply shells with desks and chairs in them. You will need to have a multitude of alternative activities available for him. When he has done a short piece of work you may allow him to go to a music corner where he can use headphones; you may have a table kitted out for aeromodelling; there may simply be a small lounge area where he can have a coffee and look through some magazines; you may allow him to go to the computer booth. It is vital for you to recognise that he will only cause you problems if he merely has to sit at a desk for forty minutes. Of course he would not be the only one to benefit from such a setting: every classroom should be designed in this way. You will find that if the facilities are there you will be able to use them as incentives for all. You will be creating a classroom atmosphere which

projects the idea that the children are there to enjoy themselves as they learn.

Group activities can also be used as incentives; they are
necessary if you are going to address the aggressive child's
need for a sense of belonging. His class group needs to be
doing things other than schoolwork—shared activities outside the usual curriculum are particularly important. Again,
secondary schools often fail to recognise this aspect of education; a fact proven by the number of pupils referred for
special education at secondary entry level.

You should of course recognise that the aggressive child
may have poor skills in basic numeracy and literacy. Many
outbursts of aggression are caused by frustration at not being
able to complete set tasks. If you take as your starting point
the skills that the child has and allow him to use these, he
will be able to do the work. If you do not bother to find out
what he can or cannot do, then you are abusing him, since
you are putting him in a situation where you will be aggravat-
ing his condition rather than alleviating it.

The aggressive child has a low level of self-esteem, and
any opportunity there may be to enhance this should be
taken. If it is possible for him to assume certain duties and
responsibilities, let him have them. Do not resent giving
these positions to him; if you are in the frame of mind where
you can say that he does not deserve them, you have re-
gressed into the position you possibly found yourself in when
you began to read this book: full of negative thoughts. As
a disabled child he needs these crutches; so long as you are
looking at his needs objectively it is possible to accord him
privileges and status without appearing to reward his
unacceptable behaviour.

You may say that to give him special responsibilities and
privileges would be seen as unfair by the other children, but
this situation can be avoided. A well-established principle
in good special schools is that whatever happens to one child
is not necessarily the best thing that could happen to
another. All children need not be treated in the same way.
They have their own unique needs and they are taught to
appreciate that they will all be treated differently. Other
schools should learn from this approach: children might then
recognise that people are individuals and begin to respect

them as such. The stigma attached to disablement might begin to disappear.

b   The Home

1   *Furnishings and Equipment*

If you are the parent of an aggressive child you will already appreciate the need to keep all potentially dangerous articles either out of reach or carefully monitored. Every home should have a lockable medicine cabinet; should one of your children be unsettled and suffer from outbursts of aggression then it is a good idea to have a larger lockable facility in order that a greater range of potential missiles and weapons can be secured.

It would of course be impossible to lock up everything that could be used in a dangerous way—it would leave the home virtually empty and uninhabitable. Aggressive children will use chairs and even tables in their rages. If you secure the smaller objects which worry you with regard to the child's outbursts then you will find that this will enable you to relax more in his presence. If you have lots of small, precious items in the house you will find yourself making unrealistic demands on him; your level of anxiety will always be a factor related to his behaviour.

Do not leave your personal belongings, such as cigarettes and money, lying around. Your aggressive child may use your cigarettes (and matches) to make a strong point in relation to his lack of a sense of identity. You will certainly know that he is around when he sets light to your mattress.

He may take your money even when he has everything a child could want; when he does this he is of course saying that this is not the case so far as he is concerned. You may think you have given him everything; he may feel unconnected to any of it. A solution to this state of affairs comes later in this chapter.

You may say that to lock away dangerous articles and to make sure that things are not left lying around is wrong in that it indicates to the child that you do not trust him. I would say that not taking precautions would indicate to him that you are unwilling to accept his problem and do anything about it. You may also say that if you took all these precautions your child would have no opportunity to learn how to respect other people's belongings, or how to control himself. I repeat to you a central tenet of this book: that *someone needs to be in charge of the aggressive child*. He needs the security of knowing that someone is controlling him; when he is ready he will maturate through this to the point where he can control himself.

Every child should have his own room in the home. He needs a place which is his, with which he can identify. He needs a place where he can be himself, away from the demands of others, a place where he can recharge himself. He needs somewhere where he can lie and do nothing if he feels like it; doing nothing but dreaming is important, since it is in this way that we start to make sense of everything. The vulnerable child, more than others, needs this facility.

Regrettably his room is more often than not associated with rejection. He is sent there when others can no longer tolerate his behaviour. You should avoid this by privately explaining that his room is where he can go when he feels himself losing control. It is an acceptable thing for him to go to his room when he knows that he is becoming angry.

If this strategy is employed you will need to equip his room in such a way that you will not find yourself having to replace the furniture every time he goes in there. This does not mean that you must buy indestructible metal beds and drawers, but that you should ensure that in his room there is something for him to do when he gets there.

We all have our moments, and when these occur we either do nothing but try to get our head together by lying still and closing our eyes, or we take our minds off things by doing something. If the child has a comfortable bed to lie on and if the room is equipped with an alternative activity, then you will find that he will not simply wreck it.

The ideal solution is to equip the room with a computer. Computer games are the best solution for these moments. Children love them; vulnerable, aggressive children can lose themselves in the stimulating graphics. In a world which ceases to threaten them they display powers of concentration previously unnoticed. They can choose their own skill levels and accordingly experience success.

Some parents would say that computer games are addictive; the same could be said about television. It really is a matter of who is in charge and whether he or she is strong enough to control the amount of time spent on the activity. The vulnerable child will not be capable of controlling himself in this regard; he will be relying on you to do so. If you think carefully, you have in computer games a powerful incentive for appropriate behaviour.

Try therefore to use your child's room in a positive way. Do not send him there as a punishment; if you send him there be sure to explain afterwards that you have done so because this is how he might avoid letting himself down. You should repeat this as often as needed. You will find that your aggressive child will begin to self-monitor his behaviour and use his room when he feels the need to do so.

If your child uses his room continually and will not come off his bed or his computer, do not worry about it. Think of the alternatives for him, and be honest about whether they might be a greater attraction. We shall discuss the importance of other activities later in this chapter.

2 *Other People*

You will know that your aggressive child can be lovable when he is on his own with you. It is when he has to cope with more than one person that he usually becomes unsettled. If you recognise this and are not always insisting that he must mix with others, you will find that the child himself will, when and if he is ready, begin to relate well to other children. Do not let your concern about his isolation place him in settings where he continually lets himself down. He may be happier on his own. A common misconception is that all human beings are gregarious, that they cannot exist in solitude. As with all aspects of the human condition, people vary in their capabilities in this respect.

It is of course important to give all children the opportunity to mix with others so that they can attempt to learn how to relate to each other. I am simply making the point that aggressive children may have their condition exacerbated if they are forced to exist in inappropriate group settings. Only extremely disturbed children are unable to relate to a person

EQUIP

YOURSELF

FOR

SUCCESS

LOOK

FOR

HELP

on a one-to-one basis; but many children find it difficult to cope with classes of more than seven children. If your child starts to be aggressive when he begins school this could be one of the signs that he is particularly vulnerable. You should let his teacher know if his behaviour suddenly deteriorates; she may be able to alleviate matters herself or she may suggest that your child be referred for special assessment.

Some children will refuse to attend school. If you sense that your child may be unduly apprehensive about this, you should prepare beforehand. Start with the principle that your child does not like change. Some weeks before he is due to start, gently introduce him to the location: take him for a walk around the school perimeter; later take him to the school gates. When he has done this a few times, allow him to see children coming out at home time. Arrange with the school for him to be able to enter the playground with you; get him to the point where the school is quite familiar to him before he has to attend.

When he does start it may be necessary for you to attend with him. If you explain his condition to the staff they should be more than appreciative of your presence. Do not hurry him into separating from you. Other children may respond to a quick and firm approach; you will know whether your child is vulnerable and the extent to which he needs to be treated differently. You may have to commit yourself considerably, but it may be the only way to avoid persistent trouble in the future.

Before taking this course of action ask yourself whether it is the child who will not separate from you or whether it is you who cannot let him go. Remember that, whatever action you take, you must have as your aim a growing sense of separateness in your child. You are trying to make him strong enough to operate on his own.

If your child has started school and you are being called to attend because of his behaviour, discuss with the staff any difficulties you may be having with him at home. Often it will happen that your child will react differently in school, so do not reject what the school is telling you. It may be possible to come to a solution if you accept that your child has difficulty in relating to others. It will also help you if you can accept that not everyone will be able to understand him and accommodate him as you do. Teachers have lots of children to look after; if you are not looking for someone to blame, you may find that they will take the same attitude; you can then examine the problem objectively and reach the best possible solution.

In the home your aggressive child will find it difficult to cope with his brothers and sisters, and having his own space will become more important the older he becomes. Usually large families have less room, but if it is at all possible, arrangements should be made for your aggressive child to have some chance of being on his own. Perhaps children could take turns at having one of the rooms; this would give your aggressive child opportunities to see whether he can begin to share.

Belongings are often at the centre of disputes. You should clearly state whether items are to be kept for personal use and only borrowed with the owner's permission, or whether items can be used by everyone with your permission. If the rules are clearly stated, then any disputes can be fairly resolved by your applying them. As always, you will need to be firm in your resolve to do this, but if you persist you will find that the aggressive child in particular benefits by your consistency.

If your child reacts aggressively to visitors do not be surprised. As newcomers they may present a threat to him. All you need to do is explain the situation to them when he has left the room. You will find that most people can understand his behaviour when it is explained. The worst thing you can do is pretend to ignore it or make excuses. If they know that you are aware of his problem and that you are attempting to manage it, they will respect and if possible help you. Immediate neighbours should be taken into your confidence in the same way; they may help the situation considerably by supporting you and understanding your child's behaviour.

3   *Activities*

If your controlling mechanisms are to be effective they must be balanced by shared family activities. When you ask your child to behave in a certain way, whether or not he does so will be dependent to a large extent on the relationship you have with him. Relationships depend on shared experiences; the more you do with your child the more he will respond to your requests. Make sure that, despite his protests, you involve him in family activities. You do not have to do things together very frequently, but if you could arrange matters so that a shared experience became a regular event, he would be prepared for it when it happened. Whether the event is enjoyable at the time doesn't really matter; its value will lie in the fact that it is something you can look back on together. Besides, while you may think that the event was not enjoyable, he may feel that it was. At the very least it will have indicated to him that you liked him and that, despite his behaviour, you were willing to make special arrangements to be with him.

We have already mentioned television and computer games. You should attempt to share these activities by asking questions and whenever possible fostering the child's interests by buying him magazines or related items. It is important for him to identify himself with some kind of activity and preferably some degree of expertise. It will be through his interest in and knowledge of a particular pastime that he will be able to relate to other children. You yourself may begin to relate to him better by taking a less passive role when it comes to his interests.

You must be careful, however, not to intrude where you are not wanted. Parents very often take everything away from a child by becoming too interested in what he is doing; they leave him with nothing of his own. Always remember that the aim with your aggressive child is to strengthen his sense of identity, of separateness. This is not easy. You can easily destroy his growing sense of identity by beating him on the computer or showing off when it comes to knowing the name of everyone who appears on 'Blue Peter'; on the other hand he may need you as a role model, or someone whose capabilities give him a sense of security. If you observe your child's reactions you will I am sure be able to decide which line to take. If he resents your intrusion you should respect his wishes. Do not become angry and resentful when he does not answer your questions; if he wanted you in there with him he would respond.

A final word in relation to activities: if you make sure that you have the day planned for your child and that there are certain events that happen on a weekly, monthly and annual basis, you will be providing him with the regular routines on which he so heavily relies. If there is a pattern to his life it will help him enormously: the more fragile he is the less he can cope with change. If change is to occur in your family routines, give him plenty of notice so that he can come to terms with it before it happens.

THE NEED FOR RECRUITS

If you are to succeed in helping an aggressive child you will need assistance.

a   To Help Professionals

1   *Colleagues*
If you are a teacher or a child care worker you should enlist the help of a colleague. You should explain that you are trying to prevent outbursts of aggression, and if your colleague is willing to help you should devise strategies that may prevent outbursts.

For example, if you felt that the child was becoming restless, you could send him to her on a coded errand, or you could arrange beforehand that she should be sent for and should come to your room for the simple purpose of creating a new focus of interest. Her sudden presence might be enough to seize the child's interest and deflate a potential outburst.

2   *Classroom Assistants*
If you have an aggressive child in your class you should ask your Education Authority to consider providing you with a classroom assistant. She could be effectively used for paired reading and general support work for the vulnerable child, or she could generally help the remainder of the class while you gave the aggressive child special attention.

Having a classroom assistant would allow you to use your imagination when it came to lessening the sense of frustration felt by the aggressive child. She could take the child or his potential protagonist out on an errand; she would have the time to focus in on him and see that he enjoyed long periods of relating to other children in a positive way. If you were to introduce her to the ideas in this book, and particularly to the preventative techniques mentioned in Part Two, Chapter 4, it might be possible for you to keep the child in your class, rather than having to recommend that he be removed to a smaller and more highly specialised setting.

Classroom assistants, if trained and supervised in this way, can be a cheap and effective method of meeting the aggressive child's needs within the classroom setting.

3 Parents

You will undoubtedly have met some of the parents of children in your class; whether you have met the parents of the difficult child is another matter. You should take the initiative in this respect, and invite them to the school—not, however, with the intention of telling them how terrible their child is and how they should manage him. They will benefit most by simply knowing that there is someone who understands what they are going through. If you support and strengthen the parents you will find that the behaviour of their child begins to improve.

If the parents are aggressive, be patient. They have agonised over themselves, their children and with professionals. You need to listen and support, not add fuel to fire. When they want advice they will ask for it, and when you give it acknowledge the fact that no one really knows the answers; one can only agree to experiment with different strategies. If you can support and recruit the parents you will find that they have great potential when it comes to effecting change in the child's behaviour.

4 Other Children

If you have a child in your class who is disabled, you will find that, if you have created the right kind of atmosphere among the other children, he will be given a great deal of support. It is a matter of your promoting the concept that we are all different and that we all experience difficulties in coping with life. Just as we must appreciate that a child with epilepsy may be excused from swimming, so we must try to understand when an aggressive child has an outburst. Children can be extremely understanding in this respect and will go to great lengths to protect one of their group members if they feel that he or she is having difficulty.

They will not take this stance automatically. You will have to explain matters when appropriate, being careful not to project a label for the child; more importantly you will have to believe sincerely in treating him as someone who needs help if you are to promote this attitude among the other children. Because of the enormous pressure he places on them they will be relying on the strength of your convictions.

If you project a caring attitude you will recruit carers; if you condemn the aggressive child he will be rejected by his classmates. A child's behaviour is affected most by his peers. If you can recruit his classmates as carers you will find them to be of enormous value in helping the aggressive child.

5   *Friends and Professionals*

You should always bear in mind that difficult, aggressive children have a great capacity to wear you down; you can easily start to get things out of perspective.

Find someone outside your immediate work situation to share your problems. You may find that someone at home is close enough to understand but far enough from your work to be able to see the wood from the trees. Do not presume that only a qualified person can help. Everyone has his own life skills, and you may find that a bit of homespun philosophy provides you with a way out of your *impasse*. You must of course keep names and details which might identify a child out of your conversation, but otherwise let it all fall out; your friends will find the intensity of your work fascinating. If they provide you with no answers they will at least have shared your feelings: you should feel stronger because of this.

If you are worried about the lack of progress you are making with the aggressive child, check to see whether you have taken the initiatives suggested in this book. If you think that you have and that the child is becoming even more aggressive, consult your headteacher. You should suggest that the child be seen by a psychologist. Matters will proceed from there. Do not be afraid to tell your Head that the child is presenting you with extremely difficult behaviour. Describe to him the techniques that you have employed so far and how the child is behaving. If you have done all you can, he will appreciate your informing him. He will not be sympathetic if it is apparent that your approach has been very limited. Make sure that you are also able to provide him with a detailed list of incidents (a suggested log sheet is given in Appendix A). This might help the educational psychologist in his analysis of the child's difficulty.

b To Help Parents

If your child is difficult and persistently aggressive, you will suffer more than anyone else who deals with him. You are the people who live with him on a daily basis; you are the ones who have to bear the brunt of his frustration. You are the ones with whom he has most difficulty, because you are closest to him.

Clearly, you need to work out a strategy for survival.

1 *Friends and Neighbours*

Apart from the suggestions already made concerning your own interests and independence (Part Two, Chapter 1), it is essential for your child's sake that you recruit help. Explain to friends and neighbours how you see your child's problems and how you are trying to help him. If your immediate neighbours understand how you feel and what you are trying to do, they will help you. If you think that they will automatically know what is going on you can expect trouble. They need to be convinced that your child needs help; you can guarantee that at the moment they will regard him merely as a nuisance who needs either to be locked up or severely punished. If you try to understand their viewpoint and resist becoming frustrated with their attitude, you will find that they will listen and eventually understand.

2 *An Escape Route*

Your child needs people other than yourself to whom he can relate. He needs someone who is less attached to him, another relationship which is qualitatively different. You will find that if he has this other person he will often behave completely differently with him or her. His attitude to you will also change. It is often the case that if a vulnerable child has the facility of an alternative relationship he will relax in his present one.

With an older child you should arrange for him to have somewhere to go when the pressure builds up. You will find that he will use this place according to his needs. Often the very fact that there is somewhere for him to go means that he is able to relax more in the home. It is only when there is nowhere to go that he will feel trapped and react with frustration. You will also be able to relax in the knowledge that when he leaves home in a temper he will not necessarily be wandering the streets.

You may consider the viability of your child actually living with someone else and coming home to see you when he feels that he can cope. There is a great deal of validity in this approach, since the family is the most difficult place for a vulnerable child to operate in. Older children can benefit from this arrangement. If you find the concept bizarre, consider how you as an adult need your parents to be close enough to visit but not so close as to be living on your doorstep. Most adults visit their parents as often as they can cope with them; after a couple of days they are more than ready to lead a separate existence. It is all a matter of feeling your identity.

3   *External Groups*

Your child needs to feel that he is part of a group other than your family, and if he is able to join a local group of some kind he will benefit enormously. You will need to recruit the adults involved before he attends. To do this you must help them understand the nature of your child's problems and how important it is for him to become involved in their association. If you are successful in getting them to understand his problems, you will be able to work out some useful strategies beforehand.

CONCLUSION

This chapter has been about sharing. You need to realise how much help you can get if you are prepared to share your problems with others.

It is important, however, that when you share them you are sharing something positive and to some extent exciting. If you can look upon your aggressive child as a challenge and can sense that the situation is not beyond hope, then you will inspire enthusiasm and support from your colleagues and friends. If you continually use them simply to moan, to exude a sense of helplessness, you will find that you begin to lose not only their support but their friendship. There will be shoulders to cry on to begin with, but they will not stay there for ever.

Whether you are a professional or a parent, you should acknowledge the fact that we all exist in a network of relationships. You rely on yours to help and support you through life, especially during the times when you are experiencing difficulty. You may need to create a network for your aggressive child. He will have destroyed any that may have existed and will be incapable of forming new ones.

Within a framework of understanding classmates and teachers he may begin to feel secure: as the adult involved it will be up to you to make the necessary adjustments for this to work. Within a supporting network of family members, neighbours and local group leaders, he may begin to have a sense of acceptance and belonging. It will take the initiative of both professionals and parents to make this happen.

3 Communicating, Consequences and Controls

Before we consider the importance of communicating well with your aggressive child and the part that consequences (sanctions) can play in making your work more effective, it is worth mentioning some other factors which must be present in the setting you provide.

1 Modelling
Whether you are a parent or a professional, you should always bear in mind the tendency of the fragile child to model himself on those around him—indeed, a feature of his vulnerability is the ease with which he can be moulded by his environment. If you take little pride in your appearance, self-care and presentation will not be important to him. If you are loud and use foul language, do not be surprised if he copies you. If you treat those around you aggressively, he will think that this is the way to behave. All children model themselves on adults who are significant to them. Fragile children do so to a greater degree since it is the most secure way of operating.

As we saw in Part One, Chapter 3, aggressive children may become more aggressive as a result of watching aggressive films; their aggression will also increase if they are living with aggressive adults.

Be very conscious, therefore, of the way you speak, dress and relate to others when you are in the presence of an aggressive child; if you are at all important to him, he will be sensitive to all that you do and say.

Professionals and parents often imagine that they need to put themselves on a child's level if their relationship is to be effective. They are making a grave error. Social workers, parents and teachers in their twenties and thirties, who dress, act and talk like teenagers, are forgetting the need for a generation gap. All children need adults.

2 Consistency

The aggressive child needs to be treated consistently. Consistency is equated in his mind with fairness and he will react aggressively if he perceives that you have not applied the given rules. You should not therefore turn a blind eye when he is misbehaving. Deal with the situation at once, otherwise the small crisis you have felt able to ignore will escalate into a major confrontation. The tiniest misdemeanour may appear trivial to you; to him it may be as significant as any other.

If you are working as part of a team you must adopt the same approach. If you see a child misbehaving behind one of your colleague's backs, you need to take action. Staff who lead teams should tell their members that they must take this approach if the necessary degree of consistency is to be achieved. They should not see such intervention as a threat to their professionalism; rather, it is a sign of their genuine commitment to dealing with the aggressive child. Likewise, parents should ensure that they both deal with a child's misdemeanours in the same way. The total setting in which the aggressive child exists, whether at school or at home, should have a consistent philosophy and approach.

3 Activities and Routines

You need to be constantly on the watch so that you can keep the goalposts in the right place for your aggressive child. This still allows you to manipulate situations in his interests and to your advantage. You should recognise the value in adjusting routines and activities in order to prevent him from failing. Having your child enjoy the experience of success should be one of your principal aims.

Activities, whether at home or at school, should therefore be prepared with this in mind. If your aggressive child is successful in an activity, whether it be reading or visiting the swimming pool, then he will enjoy it. If he enjoys it, he will want to do it again. You will have a control at your finger-tips and he will have found a way to boost his self-esteem. Prepare your day with him thoroughly; do not let it happen according to chance. Unlike other children, the aggressive child needs someone to organise things around him in order that he can work and play; if you do not do this he will become frustrated and bounce from person to person.

If you are teaching him, provide a personal curriculum; if you do not he will not understand the work, will be unable to do it and will become aggressive. It is of course important for the child to be allowed to play, but this, too, must be scheduled as part of the daily routine. He will come to see it as a recognisable activity session and may begin to appreciate that, while there are some general behavioural rules which apply in all situations, there are others which are specifically relevant to certain activities.

Parents, too, should plan each day carefully, dividing it up into recognisable periods during which different activities take place. This will help them to get through the day as much as it will help their child. The routines should be applied as consistently as possible throughout the week. Built into such a programme should be periods when others are responsible for the child, periods when a parent can go off on her own, either to rest or, more importantly, to pursue a personal hobby or pastime. This aspect of the schedule should be seen as a priority.

Three other factors in the general setting need special mention:

COMMUNICATING

A great deal of the frustration felt by aggressive children is caused by their inability to communicate effectively. We have seen how emotional fragility distorts their perception of the world: innocent comments by others are interpreted as criticism; even words of encouragement are capable of provoking a defensive reaction.

It is important to be aware of this and to understand their verbal aggression. If you speak to them and they reply aggressively, you should not interpret this as an attack on you so much as a statement from them that they are feeling vulnerable.

We shall discuss how you might cope with verbal

aggression in the next chapter, when we shall look at how you might manage an aggressive episode when it occurs.

To avoid the aggressive child misinterpreting the messages he receives from others, there is only one real solution: to take away the filter of fragility through which the messages are received. This, however, is a long-term project. A technique which can be put to immediate effect is simply to speak clearly to the child.

Expressing Yourself
To begin with you should ensure that, if at all possible, you choose the correct time to speak to him. If he is calm, and if you are giving him adequate notice of some forthcoming event, he may receive you clearly.

Secondly, you should speak slowly and simply to him in a non-threatening way. Do not be too wary of offending him, however, since he will sense any insecurity you may project. You must always appear confident in yourself: if you fear a reaction he will sense it.

Thirdly, be prepared to present the same information in at least six ways. Messages do not register easily with anxious people; you will need to repeat yourself, and for this to be effective it is a good idea to vary the presentation.

Expressing the Child
You should do all you can to encourage your child to express himself. He needs to do this if he is to begin to crystallise his thoughts; this is a necessary part of the formation of his sense of identity.

He may need to express himself in non-verbal ways to begin with, and you should provide facilities for this. Do not insist that the child talks to you or that he writes down his thoughts and feelings. Feelings in particular can often best be expressed in other ways, such as drawing, modelling, acting or computing, especially by those who have few basic skills in literacy. In every home and classroom where there is an aggressive child there should be such materials and equipment for him to use. This kind of activity is vital to him, no matter what his age. It enables him to get in touch with himself and thereafter with others.

If your aggressive child can be helped to express himself

in this way he may, with your gentle assistance, be led into verbal interaction. During activity sessions, whether he be a five-year-old doing his clay-modelling or a teenager on his computer, you could begin to talk to him about what he is doing. This will be his first step towards being able to articulate his feelings and thereafter to control his emotions.

Subtexts

Aggressive children may be extremely proficient when it comes to the use of language. During outbursts it becomes apparent that their vocabulary can be quite extensive! However, you will appreciate that when this occurs it is the subtext that you should be concentrating upon: the message of helplessness that they are so forcibly expressing.

Aggressive children can use language to devastating effect when it comes to either defending themselves or attacking others. They will use it to cajole, taunt and generally promote a hostile reaction in others. The more hostile and aggressive their language, the more fragile they are feeling.

Listening

Your aggressive child may reach the point where he begins to speak to you about his feelings. You should allow him to do this and see your role as listener. Do not be tempted to prod and probe into his past; be wary of putting words into his mouth; do not start to tell him what he should have learnt from the past and how he should alter his behaviour in the future. Provide a sympathetic ear only. A great deal of harm is done to children by parents and professionals who promote introspection. Children should be living their lives, not talking about them. They must be allowed to go at their own pace when it comes to looking at their past. The child has to feel his way into an understanding of himself, and you must appreciate that as an adult you will be capable of recognising feelings and dynamics that he cannot. If you project these onto him you will be doing him a great deal of harm; he will adopt psychological and behavioural models in his mind that will have no basis in either his intellect or his emotions. Adopting meaningless labels, he will become even more confused and arrested in his development.

NEGOTIATING

The aggressive child needs to be able to express himself not only so that he may develop self-control, but to avoid confrontation. Much of the aggressive behaviour in children is caused by inexperience in negotiating with others. Most children develop these skills; the fragile child cannot come through the process unscathed. Because of his fragility he reacts with excessive defensive mechanisms so that other children become fearful of him. He is then labelled as a bully and assumes a pattern of aggressive behaviour. Fragile children therefore need to be helped to negotiate with others; they need to be told how to ask for things they want; they need to role-play situations which they find difficult; they need to be able to model themselves on adults who, in their presence, are able to demonstrate on a daily basis how to negotiate. Learning to negotiate is, for the vulnerable child, learning how to cope with his aggression. Below is an example of how you might try to teach your child to negotiate. The approach can be adapted for any behavioural skills training you may undertake with him. The idea is to reduce his behaviour to a single skill area that can be taught.

Skills Training: Negotiating

STAGE ONE

If you are to improve his negotiating skills it is a good idea to think carefully of daily situations which seem to cause him problems and then to put these situations in order of priority. Your list may look something like this:

Parent
1 Mealtimes
2 Going out
3 Bedtimes

Professional
1 Sharing equipment in practical lessons
2 Playtimes
3 School dining-room

STAGE TWO
Picture the child in the following situations. Analyse his behaviour and prioritise the main areas of difficulty which thread through them:

1 Wanting things
2 Wanting to do things
3 Not wanting to do things

STAGE THREE
Concentrate on the priority from each list. Taking the example for a parent in Stage One, you would select the difficulty that the child has in wanting things at mealtimes.

STAGE FOUR
List in order of priority the specific skills that you would like him to learn:

Wanting things at mealtimes
1 Acquiring a place to sit
2 Reaching a compromise when it comes to deciding what to eat
3 Acquiring items on the table
4 Wanting attention: taking into account the needs of others
5 Leaving the table

STAGE FIVE

a *Explain*
Select one of these behaviours. Choose a time when the child is calm and away from others, and explain precisely how he should perform the behaviour. Do not admonish him. Assume the stance that he has not been told this before. It would not always be appropriate actually to say this to him, especially if you yourself have already told him many times, but it is the frame of mind that you should adopt. You need to assure him that, despite his behaviour, you are not rejecting him. Treat the matter as similar to teaching etiquette: he needs to know precisely what to do and what to say.

b *Demonstrate*

Demonstrate the skill to the child in private. If you have appropriate material in storybooks or on film you could use these as a basis for your approach, especially if one of his heroes is involved. If he has a hero on hand, such as one of his friends, and if his friend is a good role model, this would be even better.

c *Rehearse*

Rehearse the skill with him in private. Avoid telling him what not to do: he may well use any such knowledge to great effect. Concentrate on a simple explanation of the sequence of actions and words.

STAGE SIX

Tell the child precisely when you will be expecting him to utilise this skill. For example, rather than showing him what to do and then leaving him with a vague directive, you should limit the new behaviour to a specific mealtime such as breakfast.

Be sure that you are present when he tries out the new skill; he will need to have his behaviour reinforced. The best form of approval will be a quiet glance from yourself.

You may of course sense that your relationship with the child is such that it would be better if you were not there when his new behaviour was tried out. Vulnerable children will often behave completely differently out of sight of someone who is emotionally involved with them. They are likely to resist using the new behaviour if they feel that it has anything to do with relationships. We all know that if we can negotiate well then our relationships with others will improve. Do not, however, project this to the child as the reason for your skills training: you will be jeopardising any chance of success. Allow him to learn from his experience with the new behaviour; your task is to do this with him in private so that he can reach the point where he can implement the behaviour in public.

STAGE SEVEN

Focus on the skill for no more than a week. During this time give as much reinforcement as possible. If the behaviour is not implemented do not persist with it. Put it at the bottom of your list and move the rest up one. Begin to teach the next skill in the same way as the first. In this way you should rotate the skills to be learned. Your vulnerable child will be exposed to a cycle of skills which are periodically being presented to him; any difficulty he has in retaining information may therefore be overcome. An added benefit is that you will be able to see some light at the end of the tunnel. Each new behaviour will present as a fresh challenge; with each cycle the likelihood of the behaviour being assumed will increase.

We saw in Part One that vulnerable children become aggressive when they feel thwarted in their aims, when they feel that they or their friends are being criticised and when they perceive a situation to be unfair.

If you wish to avoid aggressive outbursts you should at all times give a great deal of attention to the way you communicate with your aggressive child. If you do not speak to him in simple language and in an understanding way he may misinterpret what you say as an attack.

If you wish to avoid confrontation, make sure that every morning you discuss the structure of the day; that at the beginning of every activity you explain what is going to happen. If you plan to go on holiday, explain this to your child well in advance; discuss with him any plans he has for the future.

Communicating with your aggressive child and teaching him how to negotiate should be seen as an essential part of your approach.

CONSEQUENCES AND CONTROLS

The central theme of this book is the need to provide external controls for the aggressive child. Feeling that somebody is in charge of his life, he may happily grow towards a sense of being in control of himself.

You may feel that the aggressive child in your life is completely out of control. In Part Two, Chapter 1 we looked at your first course of action: you must begin to feel stronger, to control yourself. To do this you must look inwards and share your thoughts and feelings with others. Before you can do anything for your child you must recognise that you are going to need other people to help you—this applies to both parents and professionals.

When you have looked at yourself you then prepare the setting (Part Two, Chapter 2) in which you and the child operate, and adjust things to make your chance of success more probable. In the present chapter we have seen how you can begin to control the aggressive child by using language to greater effect, and by recognising the need to develop skills in communication and negotiation.

It may be your experience, however, that the aggressive child can use language very effectively. Using a level of articulation that you might interpret as charm, or admire as a sign of his undoubted intelligence, he tends to control you, rather than you him. You may have discussed his behaviour with him many times, to no effect. Information seems to go in one ear and out the other. If he does as you say one moment, when the same situation recurs, ten minutes later, he has seemingly decided to ignore your instructions.

A solution is to recognise that his behaviour will not alter unless he has felt the consequences of his actions. If your aggressive child hits his brother and you verbally admonish him, he may stop what he is doing, but the next time his brother frustrates him he is likely to hit him again, more especially if you are not there. If you want your message to stick, instead of making a huge verbal issue of the matter you should calmly tell him of your disapproval. Later, when he is expecting some goodie, such as watching a favourite TV programme, you should cancel it.

Do not attempt to explain or excuse your actions, other than to say that you might have allowed him to watch it if he had not hit his brother. Avoid saying more than this, otherwise he will imagine that your decision is open to negotiation. This course of action may be difficult to take, but it will have the desired effect of driving the message home.

The message will be twofold: firstly, that he is not to hit his brother; secondly, that you are in charge.

I repeat that you should not open the matter to discussion. Take action calmly at the time of the event in order to prevent harm coming to anyone; later, follow it with a consequence.

EFFECTIVE

COMMUNICATION

AND

CONSEQUENCES

WILL PUT YOU

IN

CONTROL

You can shout at your child for ever and all you will be doing is teaching him how to shout. If you have the strength to quietly take the action recommended above, you will help him to become calm and controlled. Remember the old saying 'actions speak louder than words'. His loud actions should tell you that he is falling apart; your quiet but firm approach should assure him of your strength.

Before you can use this approach you must be in a position where you are offering the child a great deal. If you offer no goodies then, in the event that you wish to face him with a consequence, you will have none to withdraw. Indeed, if you are offering nothing pleasurable to the child he will simply not do anything you suggest. He needs to know that you are investing in him before he will pay attention to what you say.

Make sure, therefore, that in the plan for each day there is a special treat, that there is a goodie in store for each week, and that there are significant carrots in the long term. Do not use these as threats in any way. Make sure the child knows of them but do not threaten to withdraw them. When you withdraw goodies it must be done to effect and be directly related to a misdemeanour which has occurred in the recent past. The medium- and long-term carrots should therefore never be touched. They should be mentioned and left there to dangle in the child's mind. The daily treats should be the ones that are withdrawn when sanctions are required.

As well as withdrawing activities there are other actions you can take. We shall consider some acceptable consequences in a moment, but before we do so there are certain actions which you should never take.

1 Unacceptable Consequences

Children have rights and it is important to know that the following actions would be deemed unacceptable by those who protect them in law.

a *Corporal punishment*

Corporal punishment is defined as the intentional application of force as punishment. You are not allowed to slap, push or punch a child as a response to his violence.

If you are a professional you should be aware that any action which involves physical punishment is unacceptable. You are allowed to take physical action which may avert the possibility of immediate danger or personal injury to the child, others, yourself or property, but any force used must be moderate and reasonable. You are allowed to hold or restrain a child for these purposes.

b *Deprivation of food and drink*
A child should never be denied access to the range of food and drink normally available. Mealtime consequences should therefore always allow for the normal intake of food.

c *Denial of access to parents or relatives*
If you are a professional you should plan the visits a parent might make to your child. You should recognise the need the child will always have for regular contact with his natural home. You should never restrict his access to his parents or relatives as a punishment.

d *Use of accommodation to restrict liberty*
Professionals are allowed to make sure that a child's accommodation is safe and secure from intruders. They are also allowed to keep him on premises when they have calculated that he will be a danger to himself or others. They should never confine him to accommodation as a punishment.

e *Intentional deprivation of sleep*
A child should never be denied sleep. If he is awake and unable to sleep he may be removed from a bedroom or dormitory in order that others may sleep, but only until such time as he himself is ready to do so. He should not be stood in a corridor or subjected to physical activities in an attempt to tire him out.

f *Fines*
Fines should never be used as punishment for unacceptable behaviour, although a child may be fined in order that property can be repaired or replaced.

g *Intimate physical searches*
You may search a child's clothes—but this should never be
done as a punishment, only ever as a safety measure. You
are never allowed to search his body.

h *The use or withholding of medication or medical treatment, including dentistry*
You should never deny a child access to any medical
treatment.

These unacceptable consequences may seem to be unnecess-
arily stated. However, if you think carefully of your present
practices you may be surprised at how close you come to
violating the child's rights. If you are an adult responsible
for a fragile child, it is possible that you would be guilty of
doing this if you did not, for example, see that he attended
the dentist's regularly. Remember that he is in no position
even to know what is available unless you as the responsible
person inform him how to achieve access.

2 Acceptable Consequences
You should develop a system of rewards and incentives in
relation to activities that the child may share with you and
others, rather than be thinking punitively.
    You should concentrate on praising him and extending his
privileges when he behaves well.
    If you do not bear these two points in mind, then no
matter what consequences you devise for him, you will find
that they have little lasting value.
    In devising your consequences you could use the following
sanctions:

a *Suspend leisure activities*
See previous discussion, pp. 151–3.

b *Extra work*
Give him the opportunity to make up by doing work for
you. Never use school work for this purpose; you will only
encourage his dislike of it. Use instead chores around the
house or classroom. Choose chores that he will be able to
do and which will not take him too long. He needs to be

able to do them, otherwise he will not be able to assuage himself.

c *Early bed*
Do not send him to bed at six o'clock when his bedtime is normally eight: you will be placing yourself in a very tight corner. The act is supposed to be a gesture that will be of benefit to him.

If you merely wish to send him to his room, then equip it for the purpose (Part Two, Chapter 2).

d *Suspend privileges*
Whether the child is at school or at home he should be given small privileges. These will give him a sense of responsibility. He will relish them and regret it if they are withdrawn.

Whenever you employ sanctions, bear in mind that their purpose is to help the child internalise your requirements and those of society. If your sanction is overpowering and too much for him, he will see it as unfair. You will be maximising his feeling of rejection and hostility towards you. If your sanction is appropriate, then although he may protest, he will be able to make up with you by accepting the sanction. See your aim in applying sanctions as providing him with an opportunity to put things right.

3 Rewards
If rewards are to be effective they must be given when the child is behaving appropriately. I have mentioned that your day must have built-in incentives—enjoyable activities which may be withdrawn as sanctions. You must balance this provision of scheduled goodies with some system of intermittent reinforcement.

When a child is behaving well you could give him an encouraging word; you could ask him if he would like to feed the goldfish or perform some other small task which you know he enjoys; you could give him a star for his star chart, or a small sweet. You could allow him to go on the computer. You should do this intermittently—that is, not on a regular basis. The idea is that he will not be expecting the reward and that he will not be able to begin to perform

FOCUSING

ON

REWARDS

WILL BRING

YOU

POSITIVE

RESULTS

according to a set schedule. If he knows exactly when he will be getting the reward then he will be playing a game. By giving him rewards when he does not expect them, but when he is behaving appropriately, you will be reinforcing his good behaviour and he will be internalising the pattern of behaviour that you wish him to adopt.

In addition to having a list of consequences and a schedule of activities which can be looked upon as incentives, you must therefore have a list of small reinforcers which can be used in this way.

When you are compiling your lists you should bear in mind that they should be graded in relation to the impact they will have on your child. You might be tempted to use too heavy a sanction for a small misdemeanour. What will you then do when your child does something far more serious?

Bear in mind also that rewards and sanctions may lose their effectiveness if they are used too often; their usefulness needs to be reassessed on a regular basis. Each month, therefore, look at your lists and estimate which rewards and sanctions might still be worth using. Here is a possible format for you to use:

CONTROL SHEET FOR ————————————————

ADMINISTRATOR:

DATE TO START: DATE TO BE REVIEWED:

1   Incentives
    a   daily:
    b   weekly:
    c   monthly:

2   Consequences
    a   minor episodes:
    b   medium episodes:
    c   maximum episodes:

3 Reinforcers
    a   minor reward:
    b   medium reward:
    c   maximum reward:

4 Review Comments
    a   ineffective components:
    b   effective components:
    c   general comment:

SIGNATURE OF ADMINISTRATOR:

DATE:

CONCLUSION

In this chapter we began as you should always begin when wondering how to deal with an aggressive child: by looking at yourself. Whether you can alter your child's behaviour may always be open to question; you are, however, capable of altering your approach to him considerably. So look at yourself and ask some further questions.

Are you providing the kind of behaviour on which he should model himself?

Are you providing the consistency which he needs in his life?

Do you do things with your aggressive child despite his behaviour, or have you stopped?

Is your child relegated to part of your classroom or home where he is acceptable if he is unnoticed; do you only deal with him when he needs to be punished?

If you have stopped communicating with your child you should recognise that there are many different ways in which he can communicate. Bear in mind that he may have built-in resistance to talking or writing.

Have you tried explaining in a non-condemnatory way what he must do to be able to negotiate in specific situations?

Have you realised how important it is to not only to explain how you wish your child to behave, but to reinforce your words with action?

When I discussed the kind of action you might take I avoided the word punishment. You should never think in terms of punishment when dealing with the aggressive child. He cannot be held accountable for a great deal of his actions. He is emotionally vulnerable; dis-abled because of his fragility. The last thing he needs is somebody punishing him. You must always think in terms of rewards and consequences when you are trying to alter his behaviour, and you must employ them in that order. Give ample reward for his good behaviour and you may find that you extinguish that part of his behaviour which you find unacceptable.

If as a parent or a professional you find that you are unable to do any of these things, you need to go back to Part Two, Chapter 2 and recruit the help of others. They will understand your difficulty if you share your thoughts and feelings with them.

It is of crucial importance for your child to know that someone is in charge of him, that there is someone caring for him. When he has a sense of security from this he will begin to be able to communicate and negotiate. In so doing he will develop his personal controls, and his aggression will diminish.

4　Practical Matters

You may have noticed that every technique I have mentioned so far could be regarded as preventative. If you understand a little about aggression and appreciate the part it plays in the developing child and adolescent, you will have begun to prepare yourself for dealing with the aggressive child in your life—and preparing yourself is the first thing you must do if you are going to be able to prevent him reaching the point where he has an aggressive outburst.

Every time he does this he lets himself down; he confirms his experience that he is unable to control himself and the level of his self-esteem sinks lower. In a repeating pattern he spirals downwards, feeling more and more rejected. If you can prevent episodes of aggression occurring you will be enabling him to feel better in himself; you will be avoiding situations which cause both of you a great deal of heartache.

Preventing aggressive outbursts should be the central thrust of your programme. If your child can experience progressively longer periods when he is calm and relaxed, he will reach the point where he can begin to see his aggressive behaviour objectively; his appropriate behaviour will become self-reinforcing as he experiences the pleasure it brings him. So strengthen yourself, devise a personal programme for your child, prepare equipment, adjust the setting, provide incentives, rewards and an array of consequences, and you will have employed some of the most effective preventative techniques available.

However, aggressive outbursts will still occur. Despite all precautions you take you will never be able to guarantee that your child will react as you would hope. He perceives things differently from you and his perception will vary according to how he is feeling at the time. He is fragile and can interpret actions and words in a totally unexpected way. All you can do is remain strong in your resolve to help him, and consistent in your approach. When he starts to perceive the world more accurately there will be fewer confrontations; it will be a sign to you that he is becoming more resilient.

In this chapter we shall look at some further ways in which you can prevent your child having an outburst, and we shall also discuss how you might cope with the outbursts when they occur.

PREVENTATIVE TECHNIQUES

Before we begin I would like to stress a point I have already made:

Liking the Child
Before you can employ techniques effectively you must be honest with yourself about whether you have a dislike for your child. If your work with him is to be successful, he must sense that, despite his behaviour, you will still accept and like him. You will find it impossible to project this feeling unless it is genuine.

If you feel that you do dislike him, to the point where your involvement is a charade, then accept that if his behaviour is to improve he must have someone else to help him. By struggling on you will make matters worse for both of you. Parents may find it difficult to accept that their child would be better off being cared for by another person. They should see it as their responsibility to accept that their child has special needs and to recognise that his fragility may mean that they themselves are the worst possible people for him to live with. An emotionally vulnerable child finds it difficult to cope with feelings, and by the very nature of their relationship parents present him with the greatest of dilemmas: he needs the security that the relationship can give him, but he cannot cope with its expectations.

Parents and professionals who feel uneasy working with their aggressive child should recognise the contribution that others could make either on a part-time or a full-time basis.

1   Third Party Intervention
Using your helpers you can employ a number of effective preventative techniques. Here are some of the ways in which

your helper can deflect potential outbursts. Use these and
others when you sense that the child is on the verge of letting
himself down again.

a *Using Your Nearby Helper*

STANDING ORDER NUMBER ONE

1 On the message *Kilimanjaro*, delivered or telephoned,
she will come round on the pretext of wanting to borrow
something.*
2 As she enters she will project the notion that all is well
with you and how nice it is to see you again. She will therefore enter on a confident, positive note and in complete
ignorance of the impending crisis.
3 At some stage soon after entering she will make a positive comment to the child who is hovering on the brink of
an outburst. Her comment will ignore his plight and instead
project a positive image on to him. She will speak as though
she had not noticed his black mood.
4 She will take him to do something, or to show her
something.
5 If the child still needs her, she will, on the pretext of
needing help, take him with her when she leaves.
6 She will return with him on a positive note, thanking him
in front of you for his assistance.

STANDING ORDER NUMBER TWO

1 If the child comes to her with a note which says *Vesuvius*,
she will know that she has to thank him for coming to her.
2 She will also know that she has to keep him with her for
five minutes.
3 She will know that during those five minutes she must
give him a task that will make him feel good—most probably
one involving giving her help that she had been waiting for.
It will be a task that the child is capable of doing and completing.
4 She will return him to you and apologise for keeping

---

* Do not tell her specifically why you need her. She will know the
child's name and that is all she needs if she is to maintain a credible air
of innocence.

him: it was fortuitous that he arrived when he did. She will say how helpful he has been.

STANDING ORDER NUMBER THREE
1 If the child comes to her with a message which says *Mount Etna*, she will know that she has to return with him to you so that he can show her his work.
2 She will know that she must encourage him whatever the quality of his work.
3 She will know that she will need to look at other things he may have been doing.
4 She will know that she is to ask the child if he will bring the work to her, with your permission, when he is finished.
5 She will know that she must tell him how to be polite and what to say when he wishes to leave you. She will thank you for being so kind as to allow her to visit.

b   *Using Your Assistant or Helper in the Home*

STANDING ORDER NUMBER ONE
1 If you touch your helper on the shoulder she will know that she should approach the child and ask him to help her to do some chore.
2 She will know that this will involve taking the child out of the room.
3 She will know that the child needs to be given a task that involves helping her, something that can be shared with her and which the child is capable of doing well.
4 She will know that the child should not be returned to the room until he is in a positive frame of mind.
5 She will know that when she returns him to the room, she will thank you for allowing him to be with her; she will thank him for being such a great help to her.

STANDING ORDER NUMBER TWO
1 If you take your helper's hand she will know that she should approach the child and ask him to do something in the same room.
2 She will know that you wish her to ask him if he would like to show her his computer skills, his most recent aeromodel, or any similar conversation piece.

3 She will know that after a while, when the child is speaking positively, she is to link you into the conversation, by telling you directly what he has been telling her.

4 She will know that you will then leave them to it for a little longer.

5 She will know that when you return to join in with them again, she will need to leave you with the child when you give her a nod.

STANDING ORDER NUMBER THREE

1 If you say to your assistant, 'My nose is itching again,' or some other coded message, she will know that she is to sit with the child.

2 She will know that she is to talk to him about her troubles or about some sad thing she has heard of.

3 She is to ask for the child's advice or comments.

4 She is to listen to what he says and encourage him to expand.

5 She is to thank him for listening and to say how much he has helped her.

The significant factor in the technique of Third Party Intervention is the opportunity it provides for the child to have a fresh start. By the time you think it is necessary to utilise the technique he has become emotionally involved in relationship dynamics that he cannot manage. A new face on the scene allows everyone a fresh start; if it appears on the scene soon enough it can defuse the impending crisis.

2 Leaving Alone

When we discussed the provision of facilities in the home and classroom we were making the point that the aggressive child has a low level of concentration and needs to have a variety of things to do if he is to avoid becoming frustrated.

When you are providing these facilities, bear in mind that it is useful for some of them to be outside the house or classroom, enabling the child to leave the group situation and be on his own.

At School

If at all possible, you should have a weather station in the school grounds; you should have litter bins in a number of locations. You may have flowerbeds, even a small animal compound. You will have a secretary's office, and more than likely a secretary sympathetic to your aims. You will have a library and you may have a tuck shop. All these facilities can be looked upon as external resources, useful deflectors of aggressive behaviour.

Do not assume that your aggressive child will let himself down when he is sent to use them; trust him and you may be pleasantly surprised. Always ask what there is for you to lose. If you have taken the correct precautions, such as forewarning the school gardener or librarian, then you should not lose your job.

If things go wrong, you make the child wait a while before trying again, and if it is clear from the start that he will not be able to manage on his own, ask your helper to go with him.

At Home

If you have a garden or a yard, think about how you could use it to enable your child to get away from the rest of you. It may be possible for him to have the use of a garden shed or a garage; you may be able to provide him with space to tinker with his bike or play with his rabbits. You might think of allowing him to go to the nearest shops on errands.

If you feel that it is simply impossible for him to do anything on his own outside the home, think again; you may have reached a dead end on this matter: it may be time for you to ask what you have to lose if you give him a little more freedom.

If you fear that he might lose his life and you a son, then turn to your helpers. Perhaps they could take him on errands, take him to the park, or simply be with him while he plays in the back garden.

It is important for your child to have an escape route—somewhere he can go to when it is all getting too much for him. If his room is well equipped he will use this in a self-monitoring way. Remember that he needs to be able to get away from you quite a lot: you must provide for this.

3 Reassuring

Although the vulnerable child finds it difficult to have close emotional relationships with anyone, he may gain reassurance by your being physically close to him.

At School

You should make sure that the child is placed close to your work area. You should not think of this as enabling you to keep your eye on him more easily, so much as allowing him to be in a position where he can feel more secure. He will find it difficult to relate to the other children, and if his desk is near yours he will be able to relate to them at his own pace. Your physical presence should in no way be a threat to him, so do not react to his every move. If you are close to him you should be able to gauge more accurately when and when not to intervene. It is a good idea when you are at your desk to be working on something yourself and not simply sitting there watching his every move. An advantage of having him close to you is that you can pay him the attention he needs without it being so apparent to the rest of the class.

If you are close to him you will be able to reinforce your words of encouragement by touching him. If you are able to do this you can be sure that whatever you say will have more impact on him.

Your aggressive child may react unfavourably to these suggestions. He may only be able to operate when he is quite isolated from you and others; he may respond aggressively to your touch. Gauge the time when you can have him close in this way. Do not force the issue, or he will interpret your action as a sign of your mistrust in him.

At Home

Whenever possible you should take the opportunity to provide your child with the warmth of physical contact. Fragile children may respond to this but, regrettably, it is often denied them: their violent behaviour has resulted in rejection and their intrinsic fragility prevents them from achieving such closeness. However, there may be occasions when a cuddle and a hug are possible. You will know when this is the case and should take advantage of it.

You may find it difficult to express yourself in this way, but if you can look upon it as a need that your child has, you may be able to provide this very basic form of human contact for him.

Vulnerable children operate at the extremes: they will either resent physical closeness or they will suffocate you with it. If you find that your child is too close for you, that he is tripping up on your heels, you should recognise that he needs to be close and not resent it: when he feels more secure he will be able to walk and sit on his own. If he resents any physical contact you should respect this and not interpret it as rejection from him: it is a symptom of his fragility.

An aggressive child may appear to be in no need of help or reassurance of any kind, but his actions speak louder than his words. He is loud, aggressive and domineering *because* of his great need to protect himself. If he were strong inside he would have no need to do this, but he is weak and vulnerable. You should therefore reassure him, strengthen him, in as many ways as you can. Show an interest in him, in his hopes and aspirations and in whatever he is doing. Try to share his concerns and show that you care who he is.

If you are a teacher you should not simply be concerned with his classwork: you should know him as a person. If you are a parent or helper you should become involved in all aspects of him. Simply sitting and looking at a book with him, or watching television and chatting, are signs that you are willing to spend time with him.

You need to go further than this if your work is going to be of lasting value: you need to show him affection. The aggressive child does not make this easy, but you should realise that he desperately needs to feel accepted. He needs every assurance that, despite his behaviour, you accept him and love him. It is a good idea to expose him to this from time to time, particularly when you feel that an outburst is coming.

An effective way of giving assurance that you accept him is by using humour. A well-timed humorous comment might just be enough to ward off another outburst. Your humour could indicate to him that you are on the same wavelength: it could tell him that you know where he is, how he is feeling. Be careful not to use sarcasm or to be cynical: the risk of misinterpretation is too great. Be sure at all times that there is no condemnatory subscript to your humorous comment: if it is at all judgemental it will be far more hurtful to him than a simple statement.

4 Ignoring

An effective way of extinguishing unwanted behaviour is to ignore it, and the effectiveness is increased when concurrent appropriate behaviour is rewarded. If you want to prevent aggressive outbursts you should first make sure that you are rewarding your child when he is behaving well, and then see how far you can ignore his outbursts. If his aggression could be said to be harmless then it will be easy to ignore, but if he is endangering himself or others it will be important for you to take action.

Let us take a scenario illustrating aggressive behaviour which may be said to be harmless.

a *At School*

The child enters your room. He slumps into his chair and bangs his books onto the table. He avoids looking at you and when he does he stares in a sullen and resentful way. When you speak to him he mimics you in reply. He uses offensive language under his breath.

All this poses a threat to you, and your natural reaction is to bristle in self-defence. You may either counter-attack and repress the assault, or you may capitulate and allow him to take control. Should you take either course of action you will feel uneasy afterwards. If you counter-attacked you may have given him the response he wanted; if you gave in you will feel humiliated. The net result of either approach will be a resumption of the battle at a later date.

If you ignore his behaviour and bear in mind that he is acting this way because he is unsure of himself, you could take a different and more positive line of action. As he enters the room you could take the opportunity to comment on some aspect of his clothing that you like; you could ask him how the football match went the previous evening; you could

IGNORING

MEANS

PAYING
ATTENTION

TO THE

SUBTEXT

OF HIS

BEHAVIOUR AND
LANGUAGE

ask him to do something for you, such as distribute books or equipment.

You are there to improve how he feels about himself, not to make matters worse.

If he persists with his aggressive approach you should talk to him privately. Do not humiliate him in front of his peers. Explain calmly and clearly how you expect him to behave, and return him to the room.

If after three such episodes you feel that this line of action is getting you nowhere, you should examine the following before recommending that he needs to be excluded permanently from your room:

1   Your perception of his aggressive behaviour.
2   Your provision of appropriate work and classroom activities for him.
3   The effort you have made to recruit helpers for him.

You may say that to take the above approach would have a disastrous effect on the rest of the class and you could be right: behaviour can be contagious. However, if you have treated the class as individuals and become interested in them as people, they will recognise his actions as being a symptom of shakiness and unpredictability, and yours as indicative of confidence and self-control. Whether he gains the support of the group will depend on how far you have established meaningful relationships with them; this in turn will depend on whether you have taken all the necessary preventative measures mentioned above.

Notice that ignoring unwanted behaviour does not mean that you take no action.

b   *At Home*

Your child comes in from school. He throws his coat on the floor and kicks off his shoes. He ignores you when you speak to him; he turns the television on loud. He swears at you when you ask him what he would like for tea. He turns the television off and runs upstairs. He bangs his bedroom door hard. You hear him throwing furniture around and yelling obscene language at you. There is a crash and his door bangs again as he rushes downstairs and into the kitchen. When you ask him what he is doing he replies with foul language.

Your immediate reaction to him coming in like a tornado

will be to control him, to stop him physically. You will feel
like grabbing him and gagging him when he swears at you;
you will feel apprehensive to say the least when you hear
the furniture flying around, and you will be almost uncontrollable by the time he rushes down into the kitchen. When
he finally swears at you, and you have the carving knife in
your hand . . .

Such episodes occur in many households, but it is their
intensity and frequency which indicate to you the special
nature of your child's problem. What for most people are
once-in-a-lifetime crises are everyday occurrences for you
and him. The stress of attending school is released when he
returns home, and mother is usually the person who bears
the brunt of his frustration and anxiety.

As a parent it is particularly difficult for you to be objective about such episodes, and to think about how you might
improve your child's behaviour by ignoring it. You need an
immediate solution if you are to survive. You must, however, attempt to see the situation in a fresh light. You must
try to be positive, and should you have read this far you will
already have gathered that there are arrangements you can
make in your house to avoid such behaviour occurring.

During such an episode you should ignore everything and
listen to it all.

Do not respond with a counter-attack by shouting and
swearing back at him.

Listen carefully to everything that he is doing and saying.
He is venting his spleen on the world and you in particular.

Choose one single aspect of his behaviour that you disliked. For example, you may choose the fact that he threw
his coat on the floor when he came in. Work on this part of
the entrance scene only.

After the episode, when he has calmed down, talk to him
in private. Explain, demonstrate and rehearse how he should
hang his coat in the hall when he comes in. Do not be harsh
or condemnatory when you do this. You are simply making
sure that he knows exactly what you require.

The following day you could have a snack ready for him.
If he comes in and hangs up his coat properly, you could
give it to him. Do not say why he has got this small treat.
If he does not hang up the coat, go through the process

again. Repeat three times, each time having the goodies available for him if he does as you wish on the following day.

When he has got into the habit of doing this, or if your efforts fail, you could start to concentrate on another aspect of unwanted behaviour in the grand entrance scene. In all your deliberations, consider how you might adjust the setting in order to avoid outbursts occurring.

Ignoring unwanted behaviour does not mean doing nothing about it. It means responding to it appropriately. This means keeping your head and working out some way to put things onto a positive footing.

5 Alternative Behaviour

You should also provide alternative behaviour for your child to adopt when he suddenly finds that he is becoming agitated and liable to explode. Part of your work will be to help him realise, especially as he gets older, that he has a problem with his feelings. You should be able to discuss with him how he can gauge when an outburst is impending. He should be able to tell by a funny feeling inside, a general restlessness, or by the fact that everybody seems to be annoying him and nothing is going right.

When he feels this way it may be possible for him to avoid outbursts by taking certain agreed actions. In school, he may ask to attend to the weather centre; at home he may go into the garden and do some digging. We all need activities to take us through our crisis points. You must provide these facilities for your aggressive child; by using them he may eventually be able to cope with his aggressive outbursts on his own.

COPING WITH VERBAL AGGRESSION

If a child is verbally aggressive you should always try to read the subtext which he is transmitting. Essentially he will be letting you know how insecure he feels, but he may also be unable at that moment to communicate his concern. Let us look at a typical episode.

You speak to your child in a pleasant way and he ignores you. When you try to speak again he shouts at you, using foul and highly offensive language. He then puts his head on the table and covers himself with his arms.

You should appreciate that if a child is highly vulnerable he may not want to speak to you. You utter one word and it is too much. His feelings are ambivalent: he wants to unload but he has difficulty in communicating. He is upset about something, but he may not know what it is. On your prompt he explodes in an irrational manner. When he puts his head down and cries to himself he knows that he has failed yet again.

You should not expect your child always to want to speak to you; you could be making demands on him which are too much at that moment. Allow him to take the initiative in situations where you sense that he is having difficulty inside.

Do not react by hurling abuse back at him when he swears at you. Remain calm and observe the performance. If you react emotionally he will have got you performing in the only way he knows. You must try to break his habit of communicating to you in this way. If he swears at you in a group situation, separate him from the group.

After such a verbal outburst, give him time to recover himself. When he is ready, speak to him. Do not rush in with all the 'should' sentences. He will often know what he should have done; his anguish is caused by the fact that he has been unable to do it. Ask him what has happened to make him so angry. Listen to what he says. Say that you understand; listen and show that you are interested. Ask him how he thinks the situation could have been avoided; do not tell him.

In both school and home there are occasions when you cannot ignore the child's aggressive behaviour in any sense: this is when his actions are going to threaten the physical welfare of himself, you or others. We shall now discuss some possible ways in which you cope with these episodes of aggression.

COPING WITH PHYSICAL AGGRESSION

1 Review the Rules

When a child attacks you or someone else, you need to take action. If the situation has gone this far you cannot ignore it. If you do nothing someone will get hurt.

If you feel unable to intervene successfully, do not do so. You should not put yourself in physical danger; if you know that you are not strong enough to restrain him, you will only make matters worse by intervening. Send for immediate help. If you are confident that you can intervene successfully, you must remember that your purpose in doing so is to:

a   prevent the child from harming himself
b   prevent him from harming others
c   prevent him from damaging property

You should remember also:

a   you are allowed to restrain him for these purposes
b   you should use reasonable force at all times
c   your intention should be to avoid injury to the child
d   you are not allowed to attack him in any way

If you do not abide by these rules then you will be acting against the law.

If you are unsure about the course of action you are allowed to take when a child is physically aggressive you should consult your immediate superior. He or she will be able to give you access to local and national guidelines on these matters. Children suffer abuse from adults who go beyond restraining them; they are protected in law against irresponsible and uncontrolled retribution.

I do not intend to present scenarios to illustrate the following techniques. The assumption that specific advice can be given does not allow for the relationship between antagonists or those who may intervene; it cannot cater for the complex chemistry which attends each episode.

I feel, however, that it may be possible to provide some general guidelines which could apply to most situations.

2 Physical Fitness and Techniques

You need to be fit to cope with aggressive children. You also need some training in actual handling techniques. You

PHYSICAL CONTACT

1 KNOW THE RULES

2 PLAY FOR SAFETY

3 NEVER ATTACK

must know how to hold and restrain without injuring the child or yourself; you may need to know how to separate children from each other or how to defend yourself.

Training in the martial arts promotes not only fitness but self-control. It can equip you with techniques that will enable you to protect the aggressive child. If you really want to feel confident in your ability to cope with aggressive episodes then you should join a martial arts club where you will be able to acquire expert instruction. When you have acquired the necessary skills you will find that you are less anxious and more able to look at behaviour objectively. You will feel stronger and less susceptible to threat.

3 Episodes of Aggression

a *Between Two Children*

In the event that an episode of violence occurs between two children:

THINK: physical safety

SEND: for immediate help

REMOVE: all other children and dangerous items

If you feel able to intervene:

1 HOLD the main aggressor. Place your body between the antagonists. Quietly tell the other child to leave the room.

2 TALK QUIETLY to the child you are holding. Do not loosen your hold until he has calmed down. As his breathing becomes more regular, speak reassuringly to him. Do not expect him to be hearing what you are saying: your voice is to be used merely as a calming influence.

3 MAKE HIM FEEL GOOD. Recognise that the child is feeling extremely badly about himself: do not lecture him about his behaviour. Do not ask what happened—you will only add fuel to fire. You are there to make him feel better.

It will take a long time for him to recover: do not rush him. You may recover more quickly than he. Keep him in private until he is settled; if you expose him to others too soon he will react with further violence.

4 GRADUALLY RELEASE HIM as you sense his self-control returning. Assure him of your understanding. Tell him that you will see him later to discuss how he might avoid this happening in the future. Give him some immediate

instruction so that he can do something to start again, something which will take his mind off what he has just done.

If there are other children waiting to return; explain that the episode is over, and that you do not want to hear any more about it. It is a private affair and is not to be discussed.

b   *Between a Child and Yourself*
In the event that a child attacks you:
   THINK: avoid injury
   SEND: for help
   REMOVE: all other children
1   HOLD. If you are able, assume a position of holding. Your aim is to avoid injury to both him and yourself.
2   REASSURE. The child will know that he has committed an horrendous error. It is taboo among children to attack adults. He will need every assurance from you that you acknowledge his mistake, and that you will not retaliate.

Speak to him quietly; tell him that you understand. He will need you to be firm and calm. By holding him and talking to him you will eventually feel him relax.
3   RELEASE. Release him when he has calmed down. Give him time to do this. Allow him to come out of the episode in private, with no further loss of dignity.

Tell him that you will see him later to discuss how the situation can be avoided in the future. Give him something to do immediately; something to allow him to carry on.

Invite the other children in; explain that the episode is private and closed. You do not want it to be discussed.

NOTES:
a   If the violent child becomes separated from you, you should only block his escape route when it is clear that you are able to do so effectively, and when it is also clear that if he escapes he is likely to come to some harm, or to harm others.

A violent outburst can often best be resolved in private; many children will run out to avoid losing face. The best plan is to make arrangements for a specific location that he can use for this purpose.

THE FOUR R'S

RESTRAIN

REASSURE

RELEASE

REINSTATE

b   In instances where other children are present and you have removed them, do not worry about their welfare. They will be controlled by the shock of the episode. They will look after themselves until your help arrives.

c   When your help arrives you will have to decide whether you actually need her with you. It may be that by this time you have managed to restrain the child. It would be better if you could manage to allow the child to recover with just yourself. The fewer people who see him in this state the better.

If your helper is needed physically to separate two children or the child from yourself, you should make sure that at the earliest possible time one of you leaves. He will only cause you more problems if two of you are there for longer than need be.

CONCLUSION

It is impossible to give specific advice on how to deal with physical aggression since each episode of violence has its own unique chemistry.

The fear that people have when dealing with the aggressive child is caused in part by the unpredictability of his behaviour. It is therefore vitally important to consider all possible techniques which can stabilise his performance and prevent outbursts occurring.

The fear that the child promotes in people is also caused by a lack of confidence in how they might react when he becomes physically aggressive: they feel that they themselves might go out of control. Parents and professionals will know that the stress they experience during these outbursts is caused by the holding back of their natural inclinations.

Children are protected in law from adults who cannot control their raw emotions and it is essential that all who work with them should be well acquainted with both national and local guidelines. Professionals who work with aggressive children should not feel that it is enough to have good intentions; parents of such children should not feel that they are able to rely on their intuition alone. Fragile children are expert at eliciting the worst kind of behaviour in others.

5 Alternatives

As we have seen, it is essential for anyone who is working with a difficult, aggressive child to have the help and support of others. Aggressive children can place an enormous amount of stress on those around them. The 'third party' can alleviate this considerably, even if his or her involvement is limited merely to listening to what a parent, teacher or child care worker is going through.

If you are working with a difficult child you will be able to make adjustments to your lifestyle and to the provision you make for him; having read this book and noted its suggestions you may have concluded that it is possible for you and your helper to cope quite adequately.

WITHDRAWING A CHILD FROM HOME OR SCHOOL

You may feel, however, that the child's aggression is too much for you to handle, and that he should be removed either from your home or from your classroom.

Before you make the necessary enquiries you should have one last look at the arrangements and techniques suggested so far. If you have tried implementing these and nothing has worked, bear in mind that one important suggestion I made was that all techniques and arrangements should be yours: you will need to experiment with them and refine them to suit you and your personal situation. You cannot expect a technique to work unless you feel that it is your own idea. It is not possible to tell people how to manage behaviour; it is only possible to suggest approaches. One general piece of useful advice is to be imaginative. There are no set answers. Make sure that you stay within the law and, after reading my suggestions, create your own personal techniques.

When I referred to the crucial part that helpers may play

in your work, I was referring to your neighbours, friends or relatives if you are a parent, or to your immediate colleagues if you are a professional.

There are other people who may help. If you are a parent you should speak to the head of your child's school, expressing your concern and asking if it is possible for her to make arrangements for you and your child to see a child psychologist. You could also discuss matters with your local social services department (see p. 188).

If you are a teacher or child care worker you should likewise ask the head of your establishment if it is possible for you to refer the child to a psychologist.

When you make these requests you should be prepared to discuss all that you have tried to do to help your child. You should be able to give good evidence of this, and you will find it easier if you have kept accurate records of:

1   The child's behaviour (see Appendix A).
2   The special arrangements you have made to cater for:
   a   his behaviour
   b   his learning difficulties
   c   his strong points.

(If you are not sure what I am talking about, you could reread Part Two.)

Some difficult children can cope in the mainstream setting and in their homes, but they need special arrangements; before a child is withdrawn for special education or into the care of the local authority, all parties concerned need to examine the moves that have already been made to cater for his special needs.

AVOIDING DISRUPTIVE BEHAVIOUR IN SCHOOL

Teachers should be trained to deal with difficult children; training courses should embrace preventative techniques and give emphasis to the fact that teachers are employed because children need them as people. If the behaviour of children were seen as the primary concern of teachers rather than a secondary matter, then the delivery of the curriculum would proceed much more smoothly. Difficult children would not be seen as a nuisance; their needs would be met, and others could benefit as a result.

Enormous sums of money, incurred by making special needs provision outside the mainstream setting, could be saved by the requirement that on the staff of each school there should be at least one specialist who would teach part-time in a subject specialism, and in the remainder of his schedule have a specific responsibility for the following throughout the school:

1 The implementation of 'preventative' techniques mentioned in this book and elsewhere. If all teachers adjusted their facilities and curriculum so that they could meet the needs of the difficult child, his disruptive behaviour would cease.

2 Family support work. Supporting families of difficult and aggressive children can result in a dramatic decrease in the level of their disturbed behaviour. Parents are strengthened to the point where they can begin to control their children; the children feel that somebody is beginning to understand their personal life.

EXCLUSIONS

When a child is excluded from school it is usually because it would not be in the interests of other children for him to remain there; he will have committed some serious offence. Sometimes the offence is a one-off episode, but because of its seriousness it makes exclusion unavoidable. In most cases, however, the offence which results in the exclusion is the last straw—the culmination of a variety of anti-social episodes. By the time a child is excluded he will have become extremely unpopular and disliked by the remainder of the school.

It is therefore clear that it is in the interests of the child himself that he should be removed and given the opportunity for a fresh start.

If you are a parent you should never fight against a proposal that your child be excluded from school: whether there is a sound reason or not you can guarantee that if his exclusion has been suggested, he is not wanted there. You may feel that he should attend, but can you imagine how he would feel having to face everyone?

You should also realise that, despite what your child might

claim, there is a very good chance of him lying to you about the real nature of his behaviour at school. Children never like to disappoint their parents; the more fragile they are the more they will manipulate those around them.

Many children who are excluded from one school are also excluded from others. Children under ten years of age may have already been excluded from three or four schools. These are vulnerable children whose fragility has been ignored by parents and teachers; children whose behaviour is rejected rather than addressed. They feel particularly vulnerable when they are in group situations at school, or when parents make affective demands on them in the home.

It is these children who must have very special arrangements made for them if we are to avoid an escalation in the number of children being excluded from schools.

We should recognise that, with special arrangements, many difficult children can have their needs met in our mainstream schools and in their own homes. Others, however, are so vulnerable that they need to be withdrawn into special and separate facilities. Whether you are a parent or a professional, you should never presume that your child's present school or his present home is the best place for him, especially if you have exhausted the suggestions made in this book. You may be able to avoid rejecting him, if you know of other facilities which can provide a more suitable environment, facilities which you should regard as being part of our national provision for children with special needs.

SPECIAL EDUCATIONAL NEEDS

If you have arranged for your child to be seen by a psychologist, he may propose that your child has special educational needs. You may be asked to take part in a very thorough assessment, at the end of which a decision would be made about his educational placement.

ALTERNATIVE PLACEMENTS

Your local education authority should have a list of all schools approved for use in your area. The list should include not only their own schools but other private and voluntary

establishments. Many independent schools are administered
by charitable trusts and have a high reputation for specialised
facilities. It is possible that your local authority would be
willing to sponsor your child at one of these. Details of
available schools might also be found in your local library.
Some useful publications are mentioned in Appendix B.

When you suggest that a child is removed from his present
school you should always take into account what his alternative placement might be. If at all possible, you should visit at
least three schools in order that you can make a reasonable
assessment of where he would be well placed. After your
visits you may be in a position to say which would best suit
your child. Use the list of questions on pp. 189–91 to help
you decide. Your sponsoring authority might disagree, and
they may have good reason to suggest why your chosen
school is not appropriate. It is important, however, that you
reach an agreement as soon as possible. The longer your
child is out of school the worse it will be for him.

1 Home Tuition
Children are educated by tutors in their own home. This
kind of provision is seen as emergency provision only. It
may be the only provision immediately available and is particularly useful following an exclusion.

2 Day Special Schools
Day special schools offer small classes and teachers trained
to deal with children who have emotional problems and
associated learning and behavioural difficulties. They are
particularly appropriate for children who need small classes
and who have learning difficulties. Children who attend
these schools should be able to go home each evening to an
environment which is capable of providing the degree of
support and encouragement they need, and to which they
can respond.

3 Residential Special Schools
Residential special schools provide all that day special
schools provide; in addition, their assumption is that an emotionally vulnerable child needs to be in residence to receive
the type of care and consistency that only they can provide.

Some residential schools offer a small number of day placements or weekly boarding; others offer fifty-two-week provision. They are able to offer a twenty-four-hour curriculum. Above all they offer specialised help to the child and necessary respite to his parents.

Some residential schools are attached to hospitals. A child's behaviour is observed and recommendations for future placements made. Traditionally there are two approaches to dealing with difficult children in residence. Both see the improvement of self-esteem as a central aim.

a   *The Accepting Approach*
It is assumed that the child has suffered failure in the mainstream setting; that he has been unable to meet the requirements of the 'system'. He has suffered not only failure but rejection. He needs to be placed in an environment where he can sense complete acceptance; where he can begin to go through bonding processes missed during his formative years.

A safe, warm environment is provided, with few demands made on the child and with a low level of expectation in terms of behaviour and academic performance. The child grows and develops in this nurturing environment and is healed.

b   *The Expecting Approach*
It is assumed that for children to progress happily they must have rules and regulations in which to operate and a clear picture of expectations with regard to behaviour and academic performance. Exponents of this approach believe that if children know what they have to do to be good, then they can be so; they need to be provided with avenues of restitution.

Regular routines and procedures can promote not only a sense of security but a sense of achievement, especially if they are consistently employed in a small, caring community.

4   Specialists
Your child may be referred to specialists who work with him either based at home and attending sessions in a clinic, or in his special school setting.

It may be thought that the level of aggression in your child requires the administration of drugs. There are drugs available which help with aggressive or hyperactive behaviour, but because of their side-effects these should only be used as a last resort, to avoid self-destructive behaviour, or with children who have brain disease or organic brain dysfunction. It is always important to consider the medical condition of a child who is acting aggressively, but treatment using drugs rarely provides a satisfactory answer in the long term.

Specialised approaches recommended by the psychologist may include behaviour modification programmes. Aversive conditioning, cognitive therapy, contingency contracting and token economies are some of the techniques that might be suggested. It may be recommended that your child attends group session where he can be taught skills in negotiation; or that he should be provided with specialist play therapy. If you are a parent you may be invited to meetings where you can receive the necessary support and help that every parent of a difficult child deserves.

There are techniques which can be used to help with the self-management of anger. The triggers that set off the anger are examined; the feeling that is experienced and the reaction that follows are looked at carefully by the specialist and the child. Anger is dealt with by removing the triggers. This is done by the child making statements about himself and coming to realise that, where his actions are concerned, he has choice. Relaxation techniques are introduced; social skills are taught. Modelling, role play, rehearsal and the consideration of alternative strategies are used to bring the child to a realisation that he can be in charge of himself.

The techniques offered will vary according to the age of your child and the severity of his aggression. All are worth consideration. However, the talking therapies, where children are helped to delve into their past in an effort to appreciate their action in the present, are to be avoided. They assume a degree of emotional stability and maturity that vulnerable children do not have; by digging up the shaky foundations of their lives we can damage them even further. Far better is the approach whereby children consider the positive aspects of their present existence; they will then be strong enough to be able to walk into a new future.

LEAVING HOME

If you have reached the point where you are suggesting that your child needs to live somewhere else, then you must consult your local social services department. They will be able to advise you on the options available. One of their suggestions might be that your child attend a residential school. It may be possible for him to attend a school which offers a fifty-two-week placement, one which would allow him to visit you when it is suitable for you both.

Do not feel apprehensive or ashamed at having to make the suggestion that your child would be better off in a residential school. As I have explained, many vulnerable children find their greatest difficulty in the home setting. This is because they cannot cope with their feelings, and you mean so much to them. You yourself probably find it easier to manage and control other children than you do your own. In an appropriate residential school your child will find it easier to relate to people and will benefit from the full educational and leisure programmes that can be offered; you will have time to become strong, to be able to cope with him when he visits.

In deciding which kind of residential school might be most suitable for your child you should think carefully and not immediately go for the 'expecting' approach. Your child might not be able to cope with the demands that this approach could make. Do not immediately say that what he needs is discipline—that rules and regulations will be good for him. There are some children who react against this. Placed in a school where they have to do as they are told their behaviour can deteriorate further, despite the extra care and attention they receive: it can become bizarre, and they can become scapegoats.

Some children respond well to the structure of the expecting approach, others need to be accepted and accommodated. If you are lucky you may find a school that can offer a combination of both approaches. Take your time in deciding, because if you get it wrong the school may have to ask you to withdraw him. Once again he will feel as though he has been rejected.

It is important that both you and your child are enthusiastic about the placement if it is to succeed. You may find that you will have to be very strong and determined not to succumb to his homesickness during the first week or so, and if you are happy with the school in the first place this will help you enormously.

THE RIGHT SCHOOL FOR YOUR CHILD

When you are deciding on the right school for your child there are several questions that you should ask yourself:
1   What is wrong with his present school?
2   Is there anything more that could be done to make his present placement work?
3   Is there an alternative kind of school which could meet his needs better?

If you have come to the conclusion that he needs to change schools and have made arrangements to visit these, you should ask the following questions of each alternative placement:

1   *School*
a   Is the general atmosphere in the school happy and relaxed, or is there an air of tension and expectation of trouble?
b   Is the school approved for use under national regulations?

2   *Staff*
a   Do the staff appear keen and enthusiastic?
b   What is their general level of control?
c   Have they high expectations regarding behaviour?
d   Are they qualified in special needs work?
e   Are they qualified specialists in other areas?
f   Is an in-service training programme in operation?
g   What is the teacher/pupil ratio?
h   Are classroom assistants provided?
i   Are there men and women on the staff?
j   Are care staff qualified?

k   Are trained counsellors available?
l   Is the headteacher approachable?
m   Are all staff vetted for working with children?

3   *Curriculum*
a   Do all pupils study a wide range of subjects?
b   Is the curriculum similar to a mainstream school?
c   Is it possible for children to take examinations?
d   Is personal tuition available in certain subjects?
e   Is individual tuition in reading possible?
f   Do children have homework?
g   Do trips and expeditions take place?
h   What do children do in leisure time?
i   What is the philosophy of child care?
j   Does the curriculum cover 24 hrs?
k   What are rising times and bedtimes?
l   How do parents remain in contact with children?
m   What are the child care staffing ratios?
n   What facilities are there for individual counselling sessions?

4   *Facilities*
a   Are the children divided into age groups?
b   Is contact between young and old boys minimal?
c   Are classrooms attractive?
d   Are they well equipped for a variety of activities?
e   Are dormitories well presented and equipped for individual use?
f   Are showers and toilets designed for privacy?
g   Is the dining-room clean and attractive?
h   Is the menu varied and nutritious?
i   Do boys have a choice of food?
j   Is there a wide range of well-equipped workshops?
k   Is there a wide range of leisure facilities?
l   Does the school have mini-buses?

5   *General*
a   Do pupils wear uniform?
b   Are pupils expected to be polite, well-mannered and courteous?
c   Is there evidence that they can be?

d How is discipline upheld?
e Did you feel welcome?
f Do you feel that you could trust the staff?
g Would you be proud for your son to attend?
h If you were to describe the school to a friend, how would
   you sum it up?

When you have asked these questions, either during your
visit or afterwards, you should try to picture your child in
the school, and ask yourself whether, in relation to all these
matters, he would benefit from being placed there. If you
have responded positively to the above questions he will
stand a good chance of being happy there; if you have come
up with a majority of negative replies, you should look elsewhere. It is your decision.

CONCLUSION

The purpose of this book is to help those who work with
difficult children to cope with them and not to reject them.
Too often the behaviour of children is seen as getting in the
way of something else, when it is their behaviour that should
be at the centre of our concern. Their behaviour indicates
to us the state of affairs inside; it tells us how they perceive
the world and how little they feel about themselves. They
should not be rejected for it.

When a child throws a chair at a teacher it is an act of
desperation: he cannot explain why he has done it, because
it is all about feelings, which toss him about from day to
day. The tragedy for him is that because of our need to
maintain order in schools he becomes ostracised and ultimately excluded. His fate is doubly tragic when, with a little
reorganisation and planning, we know that in many cases it
could have been avoided.

There will always be certain children who need very
special provision; they will need the sense of safety and
security that small schools can offer. They will need the
specialist facilities that can provide intensive programmes
to overcome their learning difficulties. They will need the
consistency and controls that a residential school can provide. They will need to feel accepted and good in themselves.

If you are a teacher, a child care worker or a parent, you should acquaint yourself with the wide range of special needs provision in your area. Telephone the schools and ask if you can visit: they will be delighted to show you round. Become knowledgeable about local and national specialist services. It is your duty to be well-informed about every facility that might help your child. Should you be concerned about his behaviour, you will then have some idea about the alternative arrangements you might suggest for him.

Every school in the United Kingdom is required by law to abide by a Code of Practice (1994) when it is dealing with children who are presenting difficulties. It must adopt the recommendations of the Code in the procedures it employs for the identification and assessment of their needs.

It is of course extremely important for all professionals to be aware of these mandatory procedures when they are attempting to cope with a difficult child, and it is also important for you as a parent to know how your child's present school should be managing his problems. Both parents and professionals are strongly advised to read the Code of Practice on the Identification and Assessment of Special Educational Needs (Appendix D).

Unless your child's present school has undertaken the first three stages of the Code it is unlikely that he will be provided with alternative provision.

6 Towards Resolution

We began by considering whether a child's aggression might be caused by his innate vulnerability or by his life experience, and it is to this that we must now return. It may have become clear to you that your child behaves aggressively when, because of his vulnerability, he cannot cope with circumstances around him. In other words, you may have concluded that his aggression is based on a combination of his innate fragility and his circumstances.

There are many different approaches we might take when attempting to deal with the aggressive child. We can remove him from the environment that might be causing him difficulty, or adjust matters to cater for his needs. We can attempt to alter the way in which others perceive his condition. We can teach both the child and those that care for him the skills of communication and negotiation; we can devise support schemes for the child and his family. We can employ techniques to prevent outbursts of aggression.

But at any time the two inherent factors of his condition—his vulnerability and his circumstances—might alter.

It is possible to take the measures suggested in this book and alter the setting in which the child finds himself, but in essence the way he reacts to his circumstances will always depend on how he sees himself.

Perhaps we should take as our starting point the fact that we need to strengthen the personality of the child: he will then be able to cope with fluctuating circumstances in his own way. If we can somehow give him a greater feeling of who he is, a stronger feeling of identity, then he will not react so defensively to others. He needs to feel that he has something positive to offer; he needs to feel that he is unique and needed.

Long-term progress may only be possible if we can help the aggressive child to see himself in a different way. He needs to be able to look more objectively not only at his circumstances, but at his actions; by assuming a detached position he may begin to learn self-control. If we can help him to see himself as separate from both his feelings and his circumstances, we shall have done all we can towards achieving the ultimate resolution of his excessive aggression.

All these intentions may appear to you entirely worthwhile, but completely unrelated to practical work with difficult children. I can assure you, however, that before you work with any child it is vital to ask yourself what you are ultimately trying to do. Unless you know where you wish to go you will never get there; your determination to succeed will be based on the investment you have made in an ultimate objective.

In this final chapter I would like to outline a personal approach to dealing with aggressive children, and to describe an actual programme undertaken with a child. The approach utilised four principles selected and adapted from the writings of Assagioli (see Bibliography). As you read, think how in your work you might use the four principles on which the approach is based. It is extremely useful to have a broad framework into which you can thread a variety of techniques. You might also consider how you yourself might benefit from undertaking a programme of personal strengthening. A prerequisite for working with difficult children is an assessment of your own position.

RESOLUTION

To resolve the aggressive child's difficulties you should base your work on the following principles:

1 Personal Assessment
If you wish to strengthen a child's sense of identity you should not attempt to deal with his subconscious. You should instead help him to appreciate the conscious parts of his personality. To do this you can look at the present life of the child and see if you can help him to acknowledge the people who are most important to him, the places that are meaningful and the significant events that he regularly looks forward to. His personal appearance should be discussed;

friends and relatives could be considered; their viewpoints appreciated.

Your aim should be to encourage the child to look at his life objectively and to resolve ambivalent feeling towards any of its aspects. A constant objective should always be the raising of his self-esteem.

An aggressive child will always stress his failings; achieving a positive response in self-assessment may be a long and arduous task.

2   Personal Discipline

To achieve a strong sense of ourselves we must be subjected to discipline. Unless we are stretched in some way we cannot feel our limitations; if there is no level of expectation, we shall never achieve.

When we lose our will-power we become depressed, resentful and confused. A sense of will-power can come through disciplined exercise.

A child can be encouraged to do something on a daily basis. The task should stretch him and become a regular part of his schedule. Physical exercise is particularly useful. Running just that bit farther or faster than before can give the child a sense of will and determination: it is a very effective way of coming to know that he is in control of himself.

Exercise is known to promote physiological change conducive to a sense of calmness and well-being; if a regular schedule is adhered to, this in itself promotes a sense of order and harmony.

3   Personal Heroes

We all have our idea of what the perfect person, place or event should be. Regrettably these images can promote frustration if they become our real existence. Aggressive children are more susceptible than others to living in fantasy worlds where unattainable heroes fulfil their aspirations; their plight becomes intolerable when they place themselves in contrast. It is important for us all to have aspirations, however unrealistic they may be, but when dreams cause excessive frustration they should be broken and replaced with more attainable icons.

By looking at the child's ideal models it may be possible

for him to come to a realistic appraisal of what he might like
to be, how he might like to appear to others. It might enable
him to see how others presently perceive him and how they
might like him to be.

4 Personal Control
When we are strong enough, when our sense of identity and
wholesomeness is crystallised, we can move on to the final
stage leading to personal control. This involves separating
ourselves from our emotions.

We must begin to see that our self is something separate
from the way we feel, the way we think and the way we act.
Our self is something constant, which never changes. It is
separate from our intellect, our body and our emotions. It
is when we uncontrollably identify with our body, our intellect and our emotions that we are subjected to their vacilla-
tions. We should be able to disidentify at will with these
aspects of our makeup. We should be able to appreciate our
various sub-personalities.

If we could do this we would be able to avoid going 'down'
into depression with our feelings; we should be able to
accept, without remorse, our intellectual and bodily limitations. We should be able also to enjoy the rich experience
of becoming totally submerged in our feelings, thoughts and
bodily pleasures when it is appropriate to do so. It is when
we are able to make this choice that we are truly in control
of ourselves; if we can be strengthened to the point that we
can achieve this state of personal congruence, the complex
world outside will present a minor challenge.

The aggressive child will abuse this approach if it is prema-
ture. If there is a hint to him that he is not responsible for
his emotions or his physical aggression it will be counterpro-
ductive, to say the least. He will take every advantage of a
situation where he is not held responsible for his actions.
After carefully working towards strengthening his sense
of identity, working in the opposite direction must be
approached with great caution.

Before the notion of disidentification is introduced there
must therefore be an extensive programme of strengthening.
It may take many months or years before this final and exciting part of the programme can be implemented. You will

STRENGTHENING

MEANS

LOOKING AT YOURSELF

LOOKING AT YOUR HEROES

AND

DISCIPLINING YOURSELF

know whether a child is ready to begin this stage by his degree of self-confidence and realism.

If you were to implement this particular programme, or any other, you should be aware of the need to be covert in your action with a child. If you openly state what you are trying to do, he will play the game and string along with you. Your whole programme could become a charade, and of no lasting value.

You must always work to your own private aim and within your previously defined parameters; he should be allowed to benefit through the exercises you will devise for him.

These four principles should thread their way through all work with emotionally vulnerable children. Vulnerability implies a need for strengthening, and if these principles underpin any techniques which you employ you can guarantee that you will be going in the right direction. Although the following programme took place in a residential setting, there is no reason why it could not have been implemented elsewhere.

LITTLE FRED

Background

Fred experienced a traumatic early childhood. There was a great deal of instability in his family; there were many arguments, and Fred witnessed a number of violent episodes between his parents. He himself was physically abused on more than one occasion.

He was placed with foster parents, but at the age of ten, because of his tendency to be aggressive towards other children and his violence towards teachers, he entered a residential special school for children with emotional problems and associated learning and behavioural difficulties.

He was described as destructive and capable of severe aggressive outbursts. He was 'anxious' and unable to cope with other children. He could not sustain friendships. He was often in his own world, unable to express his thoughts and feelings. He thought little of himself and had been involved in petty crime.

He settled well at his new school. He received regular counselling sessions, as did all the newcomers, and over the first six months developed a good working relationship with the counsellor.

At this stage in the counselling a specific programme was not implemented. Fred was allowed to attend and not pressurised in any particular direction. He seemed to enjoy playing with the toys and was always polite and helpful. In his school work he appeared enthusiastic and compliant. He took part in leisure activities, and while it was noted that he did not like losing, he did not react aggressively. He seemed to be responding well to the small group settings and the constant praise and encouragement given to him by the staff.

After approximately six months Fred began to display his referral characteristics. In unstructured situations he was being aggressive towards other children and had begun to be destructive. He was suspected of stealing from another boy and of destroying certain articles belonging to others in his dormitory.

As Fred was still responding favourably in the counselling sessions it was decided to implement a programme.

The Programme
The counsellor showed Fred her photograph album and was surprised to see that he was interested in her background. For two sessions she used this as the basis for what she described as their first real conversation.

It was suggested to Fred that, following a weekend visit to his home, he should return with any photographs of himself and his parents that he would like to show her. He did this and for the next three sessions various techniques were used, including the making of a tape-recording related to Fred's life at home, to help him make a personal statement about his life at that time.

The counsellor was surprised when Fred overthrew her attempt to avoid talking about the past; when something jogged his memory he began to refer to his early childhood. He seemed to become withdrawn as he mentioned this. The counsellor did not press matters and Fred went on to describe the active life he now had with his foster parents. The counsellor felt that he did this with feigned enthusiasm and little genuine feeling. He seemed to be playing a role and expressing a constant desire to please.

Among the objects brought from home was a poster depicting a famous footballer. Fred was keen on football and the counsellor used the opportunity to discuss aspects of the player that particularly appealed to Fred. In further discussions she talked about the kind of people Fred liked and the kind of person he himself would like to be. Fred responded well to this but became confused when tentatively asked how he thought others saw him. The matter was not pressed.

During a further session the counsellor returned to the poster of the footballer and directed the conversation to the player's physical features. Fred was keen to display his strength. The topic of conversation was steered towards physical training. Fred was enthusiastic when it was suggested that a training programme be formulated for him. The programme would be achievable but would set him a challenge. A training chart was made and with the co-operation of his houseparent it was implemented.

Thus for a period of two months Fred was helped to realise his present identity. In certain sessions single aspects of his identity were gently returned to; he was encouraged to keep a weekly diary compiled with the assistance of the counsellor; he was helped to look at other people whom he admired; he was introduced to a number of stimulating exercises in order that he might become aware of his bodily sensations, his feelings and his thoughts. As these exercises were undertaken great emphasis was laid on the positive parts of his and other people's personalities.

Following this lengthy process of strengthening the counsellor began to introduce the idea of how other people saw him. Fred seemed ready to discuss this more fully and was even willing to consider negative parts of his makeup. It was clear to the counsellor that she would be able to begin to introduce the notion of disidentification to him. He appeared strong enough to be able to benefit from this.

Fred was asked to look at photographs of a person who was angry, sad, happy and annoyed. The point was grasped that it is possible for the same person to have many faces, many moods. He was asked to make a state-

ment about himself: on a large piece of paper, with the title
'Me' at the top, he stuck cards on which he had been asked
to write separate descriptions of himself. He seemed able to
appreciate that at the top of the card, in charge, was himself.

He was asked to find out as much as he could about his
hero figure, the footballer, and then encouraged to make a
similar chart for him. The counsellor also made a chart for
herself. During a further session she returned to his chart
and encouraged him to qualify his subpersonalities, to
describe one subpersonality and to think when he regularly
came across this 'person'. He was easily able to relate a
number of occasions when he felt like hitting someone, and
managed to think of the last time he had done this. He was
asked to close his eyes and tell the counsellor what was
happening. He did this but began to withdraw into himself.
The matter was left and the counsellor defused the situation
by asking him how his programme of physical training was
progressing. In a later session she explored another, positive
subpersonality, and Fred had little difficulty in visualising
how he had scored a goal in a recent football match.

He was then asked to return to the aggressive subpersonality, and to think of a name that he could give it. He closed
his eyes and imagined the last time he had felt the urge to
hit someone. He was asked to think about how he felt at
the time and to visualise the feeling. He pictured his anger
as a vicious dog similar to one in his neighbourhood, and
gave it the name Boxer. He seemed to respond well on this
occasion and later drew a picture of himself, with the dog—
on a lead.

Further sessions centred around the four processes of personal assessment, personal discipline, personal heroes, and
personal control. Exercises were imaginatively designed
around these four themes and employed as the need arose.
The counsellor found that a flexible approach had to be
taken to cater for Fred's varying 'availability'.

Fred never explored his early childhood, only referring to
it periodically; it was clear that he might never be able to
do this. The counsellor was pleased to hear favourable comments from members of staff who were unaware of the
implementation of the programme. Fred's outbursts had
diminished considerably in school; comments from home

indicated that he was far more communicative than before.

CONCLUSION

It is impossible to gauge accurately the success of any particular approach to dealing with aggressive children. If we were to look at the above programme, for example, it might be said that the most significant factor was that the child was receiving a degree of personal attention hitherto denied him. If we looked even closer we might say that the success of the programme depended on the personality of the counsellor and the interaction between her and the aggressive child.

All we can do is reach our own conclusions on the reason why such children behave as they do, and then formulate some plan of action. Perhaps a guiding principle is that we must become detached from him, must look at his aggression as a condition which needs attention, rather than being part of his interactional style.

It is my contention that we all have an emotional quotient: we are either fragile or resilient. Aggressive children are aggressive because they are emotionally fragile and react extremely sensitively to the setting in which they find themselves.

I hope that, having read this book, you will have a more objective understanding of your aggressive child; that you will feel stronger and more able to help him.

APPENDICES

Appendix A: An Incident Sheet

It is a good idea to keep one of these and complete it for each episode of aggression. When you decide that your aggressive child needs special attention, this will be the evidence which will support your case. It will be useful information for the specialist to whom he may be referred, and could give you good clues as to what adjustments you might make to minimise your child's difficulties.

NAME OF CHILD: DATE:

DATE OF BIRTH: TIME:

                                  ACTIVITY:

                                  ADULT IN CHARGE:

BRIEF DESCRIPTION OF INCIDENT:

Before the Episode:
a   What was the child doing?
b   Who were the other children with him?
c   What were these others doing?
d   Was an adult present?
e   Had a task been set for the child?
f   Was the child capable of performing the task?

During the Episode:
a   Did anything specific occur to promote the outburst?
b   What actually happened in the incident?
c   Did the child physically attack 1) an adult or 2) a child?
d   Did the child use verbal abuse?
e   Did the child damage or use property in the outburst?
f   Did the child deliberately hurt himself?
g   Did the child appear completely out of control?
h   Did his action appear cold and premeditated?

Immediate Resolution:

a   How was the situation resolved?
b   Did a child or an adult resolve the situation?
c   How did they do this?
d   Did the child run off or resolve the situation himself?
e   What was the child's reaction afterwards?
f   How long did he take to calm down?

Final Resolution:

a   If he talked to anyone later, who was this?
b   How did the child see the incident starting?
c   Did he recognise that he had lost control?
d   If he was full of remorse, was this genuine?
e   What plans were made to avoid the situation recurring?

Appendix B: Sources of Information and Help

1 How to Find Special Schools in the UK
In the first instance you should consult your local education authority, especially if they are to pay for your child's education. If you do not know their address you can find this in the first publication listed below. In this book you will find not only the address of your education authority, but the names of special educational needs personnel; educational psychologists and other specialists are also listed for your area.

You may not be happy with the special schools provided by your local education authority; you have every right to ask them to sponsor your child at an independent special school of your choice. These independent schools often have well qualified staff and fine facilities. Because of their independence they have been able to develop innovative programmes. Do not hesitate to telephone the schools for an appointment: they welcome visitors with no obligation for a placement to be made. They are listed in all three publications.

You will need to justify your request for a particular school and for this purpose you should use the suggested list of questions in Part Two, Chapter 5. Take the question list with you when you visit a school, whether it is independent or not, and do not be afraid to use it.

The following publications should all be available in your local public library. They contain not only lists of schools but details of other organisations which may help you.

The Education Authorities Directory and Annual (Current Year)
The School Government Publishing Company Ltd, Darby

House, Bletchingly Road, Mersham, Redhill, Surrey, RH1 3DN.
ISBN 0 900640 31 6
ISBN 0 900640 32 4
ISSN 0070-9131

Special Schools in Britain (Current Year)
Network Publishing Ltd, Palmer House, Palmer Lane, Coventry, CV1 1FN.
ISBN 0 897759 02 9
ISSN 0968 1477

Which School? For Special Needs (Current Year)
John Catt Educational Ltd, Great Glemham, Saxmundham, Suffolk, IP17 2DH.
ISBN 0 869863 25 9
ISSN 0965-1004

2   Looking for Children's Homes and Any Kind of Help
The address of your local social services, and much more, can be found in the following publication. Important contact names as well as addresses and telephone numbers are given; addresses of all manner of voluntary organisations working to help others are also listed.

Social Services Year Book (Current Year)
Editor: Kate Lodge.
Longman Industry and Public Service Management, Longman Group U.K. Ltd, 6th Floor, Westgate House, The High, Harlow, Essex, CM20 1YR.
ISBN 0 582 07869 5
ISSN 0307-093X

3   Finding Help in a Crisis
The following organisations may be particularly useful to parents who are experiencing crises with their children:

Parentline
Hayfa House, 57 Hart Road, Thundersley, Essex, SS7 3PD.
Tel: 01268 757007

Parent Network
44–46 Caversham Road, London, NW5 2DS.
Tel: 0171-485 8535

Appendix C: Select Reading List

These books will help you to cope with your aggressive child: they will provide you with a better understanding of his behaviour; some may provide you with useful techniques. The more you read around the subject the stronger you will be for him.

1 To Understand Yourself
Looking Out, Looking In: interpersonal communication, R. B. Adler and N. Towne. Holt Rhinehart & Winston Inc., London.
Encounters with the Self, D. Hamacheck. Holt Rhinehart & Winston Inc., London.
Live and Learn, G. Claxton. Open University Press, Milton Keynes.
People Skills, R. Bolton. Simon & Schuster, Australia.
Stress in Your Life, Ken Powell. Thorson, Wellingborough, Northamptonshire.
Teaching and Stress, Ed: Cole and Walker. Open University Press, Milton Keynes.
What We May Be, P. Ferrucci. Turnstone Press, London.
Human Relationship Skills, R. Nelson Jones. Cassell, London.

2 To Understand Him
Human Aggression, A. Storr. Penguin Books, Harmondsworth, Middlesex.
The Needs of Children, M. K. Pringle. Hutchinson, London.
Children in Conflict, H. R. Reinert and A. Huang. Merrill, London.
Learning Disabilities, S. Farnham-Diggory. Fontana/Open Books, London.
The Self Concept, R. B. Burns. Longman, Harlow, Essex.
Human Relations in Education, E. Hall and C. Hall. Routledge, London.

The Bullying Problem: how to deal with difficult children, A. Train. Human Horizons Series, Souvenir Press, London.

3   To Help You in Your Work
Assessing Child and Adolescent Disorders, M. Hoghughi. Sage, London.
Treating Problem Children, M. Hoghughi. Sage, London.
Effective Classroom Management, R. Laslett and C. Smith. Croom Helm, London.
Gamester's Handbook, D. Brandes and H. Philips. Stanley Thornes, Cheltenham, Glos.
Gamester's Handbook Two, D. Brandes. Stanley Thornes, Cheltenham, Glos.
Behaviour Can Change, E. V. S. Westmacott and R. J. Cameron. Macmillan Education, London.
He Hit Me Back First, E. D. Fugitt. Jalmar Press, California.
100 Ways to Enhance Self Concept in the Classroom, J. Canfield and H. C. Wells. Prentice Hall International, London.
Teaching Social Skills to Children, Ed: G. Coutledge and J. F. Milburn. Pergamon Press, Oxford.
The Joy of Learning, D. Whitmore. Crucible Press, Wellingborough, Northants.
Towards Better Behaviour, Jolly and McNamara. 45, Marina Drive, Fulwood, Preston, Lancs, PR2 4SB.
The Children Act 1989: Guidance Documents (1991). H.M.S.O. Publications, P.O. Box 276, London SW8 5DT.
Guidance on Permissible Forms of Control in Children's Residential Care (1993). Department of Health, Richmond House, 79 Whitehall, London SW1A 2NS.

4   To Help You Understand How his School Should Identify and Assess his Needs
Code of Practice on the Identification and Assessment of Special Educational Needs (1994). DFE Central Office of Information (see Appendix D).

Appendix D: Code of Practice

If you are a parent of a child whose behaviour gives cause for concern, you should be aware of the Code of Practice which must now be adopted by all UK schools when a child is presenting difficulties.

Before going to see your child's teacher, it would be useful to read an outline of the various stages of identification and assessment of children who may have Special Educational Needs.

Whether you are a parent or a professional, you will find a wealth of useful information in relation to the Code of Practice in *Supporting Learning in the Primary School* by Alec Webster and Valerie Webster with Cliff Moon and Annie Warwick. Avec Designs Ltd, PO Box 709, Bristol BS99 1GE. The following extract is taken from this very helpful publication:

SUMMARY OF STAGES IN THE NEW CODE OF PRACTICE

Stage 1: gathering information, initial identification and registration of a child's SEN, and increased differentiation in the ordinary classroom
- responsibility for assessing children, differentiating teaching and devising appropriate plans remains with the class or subject teachers.
- trigger for Stage 1 is when a teacher, parent or other professional gives evidence of concern.
- class teacher must inform the head teacher, parents and SEN coordinator, who registers the child's SEN.
- parents' and child's own views on their difficulties must be sought.
- any known health or social problems are detailed, together with profiles of achievement, National Curriculum Attainments and any other test data.

- class teacher can ask for help from school SEN co-ordinator, school doctor, other professional agency.
- support services (such as teacher of the deaf) can be called in from Stage 1 onwards, and always at Stage 3.
- record must be kept of nature of concern, action taken, targets set and when progress will be reviewed (within a term or six months, with parents kept informed).
- Stage 2 is reached if, after two reviews at Stage 1, special help has not resulted in satisfactory progress.

Stage 2: seeking further advice and/or the creation of an Individual Education Plan (IEP)
- school SEN coordinator takes the lead in assessing the child's learning difficulty, planning, monitoring and reviewing arrangements made.
- SEN coordinator seeks additional data from health, social services or other agencies and agrees appropriate action with parents and the child's teachers.
- IEP drawn up, setting out specific learning targets, using materials and resources within the normal classroom setting.
- IEP sets out nature of the child's difficulties, any special provision, staff involved including frequency of support, help from parents at home, targets to be achieved in a given time, monitoring and assessment arrangements, arrangements and date for review.
- parents should be invited to a review of Stage 2, which might take place within a term; talk to parents in person if considering moving a child to Stage 3.

Stage 3: school calls on outside specialist help
- responsibility for pupils with special needs is shared between the school SEN coordinator, class or subject teachers, and outside support services (such as visiting teachers or educational psychologists).
- new IEP drawn up including input from support services, detailing new targets and teaching strategies, monitoring and review arrangements.
- external agencies (such as teacher of visually impaired) may offer classroom support, advice on materials, technology or classroom management, or direct teaching.

– review organised by the SEN coordinator within a term, including parents, focusing on progress made, effectiveness of the IEP, any updated information and future plans.
– after review the Headteacher considers referring the child to the LEA for a statutory assessment.
– LEA will require a range of written information and evidence to support the referral (educational and other developmental profiles, views of the parent and child, health and social factors).

Stage 4: statutory assessement

– needs of the great majority of children should be met under the first three Stages, with perhaps only 2 per cent of children being put forward for statementing.
– children may be brought to the LEA's attention for formal assessment by a number of routes, such as parental request, school referral or request from another agency.
– schools must demonstrate that child's needs remain so substantial that they cannot be met from the resources 'ordinarily available'.
– exceptionally, e.g. diagnosis of a major sensory impairment, may lead immediately to referral to the LEA for a multidisciplinary assessment.
– new Code sets out criteria for making statutory assessments, a timetable of 26 weeks for carrying out the whole process from start to finish, and the procedures which should be followed.
– local moderation groups may be set up to ensure consistency and fairness within an LEA.
– evidence required for statementing includes a wide spectrum of academic, social and emotional factors.

Stage 5: statementing

– statementing proceeds when LEA is satisfied that the child's needs are significant and/or complex; have not been met by measures taken by the school; or may call for resources which cannot 'reasonably be provided' within the budgets of mainstream schools in the area.
– statement is means of access to extra resources.

– provides a precise educational prescription for the child, based on an accurate and detailed account of needs.
– parental preferences must be taken into account and arrangements made for reviews.

Bibliography

Adler, R. B. and Towne, N. (1975). *Looking Out, Looking In*. Holt Rhinehart & Winston, New York.

Ansbacher, H. L. and Ansbacher, R. R. (eds.). *The Individual Psychology of Alfred Adler: a systematic presentation of a selection of his writings*. Basic Books, New York.

Assagioli, R. (1975). *Psychosynthesis*. Turnstone Press, London.

Averill, J. P. (1982). *Anger and Aggression: an essay on emotions*. Springer-Verlag, New York.

Bandura, A. (1973). *Aggression: a Social Learning Analysis*. Prentice Hall, Englewood Cliffs N. J.

Bee, H. (1969). *The Developing Child*. Harper & Row, New York.

Berkowitz, L. (1962). *Aggression: a Social Psychology Analysis*. McGraw Hill, New York.

Bettleheim, B. (1987). *The Good Enough Parent*. Thames & Hudson, London.

Blanchard, D. C. and Blanchard, R. J. (1984). Affect and Aggression: an animal model applied to human behaviour, in R. J. Blanchard and D. C. Blanchard (eds.), *Advances in the Study of Aggression* vol. 1. Academic Press, Orlando.

Blos, P. (1979). *The Adolescent Passage: Developmental Issues*. New York University Press.

Buss, A. H. (1961). *The Psychology of Aggression*. Wiley, New York.

Cornish, D. B. and Clarke, R. U. G. (1975). *Residential Treatment and its Effects on Delinquency*. H.M.S.O., London.

Creighton, S. J. (1987). Quantitative Assessment of Child Abuse, in P. Mahler (ed.), *Child Abuse: an Educational Perspective*. Blackwell, Oxford.

DeCecco, J. P. and Richards, A. K. (1974). *Growing Pains*.

Uses of School Conflict. Aberdeen Press, New York.

Delgado, J. M. R. (1969). Physical Control of the Mind, in R. N. Ashen (ed.), *World Perspective Series*. Harper & Row, New York.

Dobash, R. E. and Dobash, R. (1980). *Violence Against Wives—a case against Patriarchy*. Open Books, London.

Dollard, J., Miller, N. E., Mower, Q. H., Sears, G. H. and Sears, R. R. (1939). *Frustration and Aggression*. Yale University Press, New Haven.

Ferguson, F. J. and Rule, B. G. (1983). An attributable perspective on anger and aggression, in R. G. Green and E. L. Donnerstein (eds.), *Aggression: Theoretical and Empirical Reviews* vol. 1. Academic Press, New York.

Feshback, S. (1970). Aggression, in P. H. Mussen (ed.), *Carmichael's Manual of Child Psychology* vol. 2. Wiley, New York.

Freud, S. (1886–1939). *Standard Edition of the Complete Psychological Works of Sigmund Freud*, J. Strachey (ed.). Hogarth Press, London.
Character and Anal Eroticism, S.E. vol. 9 (1908).
On Narcissism, S.E. vol. 14 (1914).
Beyond the Pleasure Principle, S.E. vol. 18 (1920).
Civilisation and its Discontents, S.E. vol. 21 (1930).

Freud, S. (1953). *A General Introduction to Psychoanalysis*. Permabooks, New York.

Fromm, E. (1960). *The Fear of Freedom*. Holt Rhinehart & Winston, New York.

Fromm, E. (1971). *The Sane Society*. Routledge, London.

Fromm, E. (1987). *The Anatomy of Human Destructiveness*. Pelican Books, London.

Funkenstein, D. H., King, S. H. and Drolett, M. E. (1957). *Mastery of Stress*. Harvard Press, Cambridge, Mass.

Erikson, E. H. (1968). *Identity, Youth and Crisis*. W. W. Norton, New York.

Gelles, R. J. (1977). *Family Violence*. Sage Publications, London.

Gelles, R. J. (1987). *The Violent Home*, 2nd ed. Sage, Beverley Hills.

Gelles, R. J. and Cornell, J. (1985). *Intimate Violence in Families*. Sage, Beverley Hills.

Gill, D. (1978). Societal Violence in Families, in J. M. Eekelar and S. N. Katz (eds.), *Family Violence*. Butterworth, Toronto.

Goffman, E. (1968). *Asylums: an essay on the social situation of mental patients and other inmates*. Pelican Books, Harmondsworth, Middlesex.

Golding, J. and Rush, D. (1986). Temper Tantrums and Other Behavioural Problems, in N. R. Butler and J. Golding (eds.), *From Birth to Five*. Pergamon, Oxford.

Greiger, R. (1982). Anger Problems, in R. Greiger and I. Z. Greiger (eds.), *Emotional Disturbance*. Human Sciences Press, New York.

Hall, E. and Hall, C. (1988). *Human Relations in Education*. Routledge, London.

Hoghughi, M. (1988). *Treating Problem Children*. Sage, London.

Horrocks, J. E. (1976). *The Psychology of Adolescence*. Houghton Mifflin, Boston, Mass.

Howells, K. (1989). Anger Management Methods in Relation to the Prevention of Violent Behaviour, in J. Archer and K. Brown (eds.), *Human Aggression*. Routledge, London.

James, W. (1891). *Principles of Psychology*. Holt Rhinehart & Winston, New York.

Jersild, A. J., Brook, J. S. and Brook, D. W. (1978). *The Psychology of Adolescents*. Macmillan, New York.

Kempe, C. H. and Helfer, R. E. (1972). *The Battered Child and his Family*. University of Chicago Press, Chicago.

Klein, M. (1957). *Envy and Gratitude*. Tavistock, London.

Kohlberg, L. (1984). *Essays in Moral Development*, vol. 2: The Psychology of Moral Development. Harper & Row, San Francisco.

Laslett, R. (1977). *Educating Maladjusted Children*. Staples Press, London.

Lewin, K. (1936). *Principles of Topological Psychology*. McGraw Hill, New York.

Lorenz, K. (1964). Ritualised Aggression, in J. D. Carthy and F. J. Ebling (eds.), *The Natural History of Aggression*. Academic Press, New York.

Lorenz, K. (1966). *On Aggression*. Methuen, London.

Manning, M. and Sluckin, P. (1984). The Function of

Aggression in the Pre-School and Primary Years, in N. Frude and H. Gault (eds.), *Disruptive Behaviour in Schools*. J. Wiley, New York.

Marcia, J. E. (1980). Identity in Adolescence, in J. Edelson (ed.), *Handbook of Adolescent Psychiatry*. J. Wiley, New York.

Mannings, M., Heron, J. and Marshall, J. (1978). Styles of Hostility and Social Interaction at Nursery, at School, at Home, in L. A. Herson, M. Berger, and D. Shaffer, *Aggression and Anti-Social Behaviour in Childhood and Adolescence*. Pergamon, Oxford.

Mark, V. H. and Ervin, F. R. (1970). *Violence and the Brain*. Harper & Row, New York.

Marcuse, H. (1970). *One-Dimensional Man*. Pelican Books, Harmondsworth, Middlesex.

McDougall, W. (1923). *An Introduction to Social Psychology*. Methuen, London.

McDougall, W. (1932). *The Energies of Man: a Study of the Fundamentals of Dynamic Psychology*. Scribners, New York.

Magagee, E. I. (1984). Recent Research on Over-Controlled and Under-Controlled Personality Patterns Among Violent Offenders, in I. Jacks and S. G. Cox (eds.), *Psychological Approach to Crime and Its Correction*. Nelson, Hall, Chicago.

Miller, N. (1975). *Battered Spouses*. Bell & Sons, London.

Mitchell, J. J. (1974). *Human Life: The Early Years*. Holt Rhinehart & Winston, Montreal.

Mitchell, A. R. K. (1978). *Violence in the Family*. Wayland, Hove, Sussex.

Nelson, J. and Newson, E. (1976). Day to Day Aggression Between Parent and Child, in N. Tuth (ed.), *Violence*. H.M.S.O., London.

Novaco, R. W. (1978). Anger and Coping with Stress, in J. P. Foreyt and D. P. Rattjen (eds.), *Cognitive Behaviour Therapy*. Penguin, New York.

Ollman, B. (1973). *Alienation. Marx's Conception of Man in Capitalist Society*. Pelican Books, Harmondsworth, Middlesex.

Olweus, D. (1984). Development of Stable and Aggressive Reaction Patterns in Males, in R. J. Blanchard and D. C.

Blanchard (eds.), *Advances in the Study of Aggression* vol. 1. Academic Press, Orlando.

Parke, R. D. and Slaby, R. G. (1983). Aggression: a Multilevel Analysis, in P. H. Mussen and E. H. Hetherington, *Handbook of Child Psychiatry*. Wiley, New York.

Pizzey, E. (1974). *Scream Quietly or the Neighbours Will Hear*. Penguin Books, Harmondsworth, Middlesex.

Redl, F. and Wineman, D. (1965). *Controls From Within*. Free Press, New York.

Renvoize, J. (1975). *Children in Danger*. Pergamon, Oxford.

Renvoize, J. (1978). *Web of Violence: a Study of Family Violence*. Routledge & Kegan Paul, London.

Rice, F. P. (1975). *The Adolescent Developing Relation and Culture*. Allwyn, Boston.

Ridgeway, R. (1965). *Aggression in Youth*. Priory Press, Chicago.

Roe, M. C. (1965). *Survey into Progress of Maladjusted Children*. I.L.E.A., London.

Rogers, C. (1967). *On Becoming a Person*. Constable, London.

Scott, J. P. (1978). *Aggression*. University of Chicago Press, Chicago.

Sears, R. R., Malcolm, E. and Levin, H. (1957). *Patterns of Child Rearing*. Row Peterson, Evanston, Illinois.

Sinclair, I. A. C. (1971). *Hostels for Probationers*. H.M.S.O., London.

Skimmer, A. E. and Castle, R. L. (1969). *78 Battered Children: a Retrospective Study*. N.S.P.C.C., London.

Skinner, B. F. (1968). *Science and Human Behaviour*. Macmillan, New York.

Storr, A. (1968). *Human Aggression*. Penguin Books, Harmondsworth, Middlesex.

Strauss, M. A. (1978). Wife Beating: How Common and Why, in J. M. Eekelaar and S. N. Katz (eds.), *Family Violence*. Butterworth, Toronto.

Thompson, C. M. (1964). *Interpersonal Psychoanalysis*. Basic Books, New York.

Train, D. W. (1992). *The Ideal Olympics*. Unpublished paper. Fladbury, Worcester.

Turner, C. W., Cole, A. M. and Cerro, D. S. (1984). Contribution of aversive experiences to robbery and homicide; a demographic analysis, in R. M. Kaplan, V. J. Kowenci and R. W. Novaco (eds.), *Aggression in Children and Youth*. Sijthoff, The Hague.

Warnock, M. (1981). *Special Educational Needs*. Report of the House of Commons Select Committee into the Education of Handicapped Children and Young People. H.M.S.O., London.

Wedge, P. and Essen, J. (1973). *Born to Fail*. Arrow Books, London.

Wedge, P. and Essen, J. (1983). *Children in Adversity*. Pan Books, London.

White, B. L., Kaban, S., Attanucci, J. and Shapiro, B. (1978). *Experience and Environment: Major Influences on the Development of the Young Child* vol. 2. Prentice Hall, Englewood Cliffs.

Winnicott, D. W. (1958). Aggression in Relation to Emotional Development, in *Collected Papers*. Tavistock, London.

Wolfe, M. M., Philipps, E. C. and Fixen, D. L. (1975). *Achievement Place Phase 2. Final Report*. Dept. of Human Development, University of Kansas.

Yule, W. (1978). Behavioural Treatment of Children and Adolescents with conduct disorders, in L. A. Herson, M. Berger and D. Shaffer, *Aggression and Anti-Social Behaviour in Childhood and Adolescence*. Pergamon, Oxford.

Index